SET YOUR OWN SALARY

SET YOUR OWN SALARY

A Guide to Entrepreneurship
and Financial Independence

Clinton E. Day

*BOOK*LOGIX®
Alpharetta, GA

This book represents the latest thinking in entrepreneurship and is based on personal experience starting three small businesses. It is intended for informational purposes only and should not substitute for advice from licensed professionals, who are the reader's best source for legal and financial decisions.

ISBN: 978-1-61005-628-1

10 9 8 7 6 5 4 3 2   0 8 1 4 2 5

Printed in the United States of America

∞This paper meets the requirements of ANSI/NISO Z39.48-1992 (Permanence of Paper)

This book is dedicated to two great entrepreneurs:
Curtis, my father, and Donna, my wife.

Even the most complex can be solved, but not at all without even trying.

— sarvottam

CONTENTS

ACKNOWLEDGMENTS

Thanks to my mentors who made the journey possible.

AN ODE TO ENTREPRENEURSHIP

The value of entrepreneurs to the United States economy and to society, in general, is incalculable yet not fully recognized. After all, these are the people whose ideas continuously produce better products and services, fight hunger and disease, and push the boundaries of technology. Simply put, entrepreneurs create value through disruption of traditional business models. It is the collective energy of entrepreneurs' "anything is possible" attitude that keeps the US at the forefront of world markets. Equally as important, entrepreneurs power job creation and economic growth, thereby inspiring optimism and motivation for others. In the words of Peter Drucker, who is considered by academics the founder of modern management, "The entrepreneur always searches for change, responds to it, and exploits it as an opportunity."[1]

A majority of today's millennials have expressed a desire to one day start a business. The good news is research has shown entrepreneurs are made, not born. Many individuals spend years as apprentices before striking out on their own. In Malcolm Gladwell's *Outliers: The Story of Success*, Gladwell writes that he believes the key to achievement in any field is a matter of practicing a task for 10,000 hours. Experience not only allows a person to acquire know-how, it establishes a network of contacts, all of which increase the odds in his favor. Successful entrepreneurs learn to see opportunities where others do not, and they learn to tolerate calculated risks. Without the dynamic of constant innovation provided by entrepreneurs, the US economy—even culture—would lose global prominence.

---

[1] Peter F. Drucker, *Innovation and Entrepreneurship: Practice and Principles*, (New York: HarperBusiness, 1993), 33.

Entrepreneurs also find their drive in a desire to achieve in addition to making money, and once they attain prosperity, entrepreneurs are generous givers who donate twice as much as people of equal wealth earned other ways.[2]

The story of Ewing Marion Kauffman provides a great example. He started a pharmaceutical company in his basement, which he grew into a $3 billion company. When Merrell—the well-known pharmaceutical and chemical company—acquired Marion Kauffman's company, the sale instantly created 300 millionaires. Today, the Kauffman Foundation is the largest foundation in the US focusing on entrepreneurship. Kauffman spoke for many entrepreneurs when he said, "I think the greatest satisfaction I have had, personally, is helping others, doing something that either inspires them or aids them to develop themselves in their future lives so they'll not only be a better person but be a better productive citizen of the United States."[3]

In these pages you will find a winning formula for self-employment, learn from the experience of other entrepreneurs, and discover the best methods to start a new venture. Follow these guidelines, stay the course, and you will be rewarded with financial independence and immense satisfaction.

[2] The Fidelity Charitable Gift Fund, "Entrepreneurs Are More Likely to Give to Charity," 2010, http://www.fidelitycharitable.org/about-us/news/11-12-2010.shtml.
[3] Ewing Marion Kauffman Foundation, "Our Founder," 2015, http://www.kauffman.org/who-we-are/our-founder-ewing-kauffman.

CHAPTER ONE

Build Desire

For successful people, intense, burning desire is a habit, a way of life, and a deliberate course of action.

— Paul J. Meyer
Success Magazine

All entrepreneurs start with desire. As the great success writer Napoleon Hill wrote over seventy years ago, "If you truly desire money so keenly that your desire is an obsession, you will have no difficulty in convincing yourself that you will acquire it."[4] If a person does not have the drive to overcome obstacles, success will not happen. Desire motivates people to action, produces restless energy, and pushes them to high achievement.

The United States' capitalistic economy lays a road at the door for anyone willing to take a chance on a new venture. We live in a free market system that encourages entrepreneurship and the more we like an idea, the better and easier it is to make entrepreneurship happen. Bill Gates loved computers and programming, Henry Ford tinkered happily for hours on engines, and Richard Branson saw creative work as nothing more than play. Desire is a longing or craving for something that brings satisfaction, especially when the making of money is combined with helping society.

Desire motivates a person to act, to persist through hard times, and to become more creative. It is essential to innovation because entrepreneurs ultimately do something they want to do. Eagerness to accomplish a project or follow through on an idea helps solve problems and keeps entrepreneurs

---

[4] Napoleon Hill, *Think and Grow Rich*, (Radford, VA: Wilder Publications, 2007), 23.

focused on a task. Think back to those activities and experiences in your own life that brought you pleasure and ask if your inclination or wish to engage in the action didn't help make it successful. Imagine feeling the same way about your daily work, wanting to get up and get busy doing the activities that bring you joy. Most great achievements begin in the mind of the originator as an emotional desire. Steve Jobs wanted beautiful and functional devices, Ray Kroc wanted the McDonald brothers' restaurant formula multiplied across the United States, and Thomas Edison worked through countless experiments to find a light filament that would stay lit.

As a starting point, ask yourself: What do you like to do? What do you enjoy and find easier to do than most people do? When you dream about free time, what kinds of things are you fantasizing about? Entrepreneurs who do something they love, and do it easily, are more likely to be successful than those who don't have their hearts in their ventures; however, some people develop enthusiasm in their work and get creative about their desire *after* they are underway.

Take Fred DeLuca, the co-founder of the Subway restaurant chain, one of my favorite examples. When DeLuca was seventeen years old, he wanted to become a doctor. His friend, Dr. Peter Buck, helped him start a sandwich shop named "Pete's Super Submarines" in Bridgeport, Connecticut, so that Fred could earn enough money to get through medical school. Knowing he needed money to finance the first shop, Dr. Buck provided DeLuca with $1,000 in capital, and DeLuca honored him by naming the first shop after Dr. Buck. From the outset, the plan was to offer healthier, less fattening food.

The first few Subway stores were not profitable. In fact, early on DeLuca could barely afford the $25 lawyer's fee needed to sign his lease. DeLuca explains that he was hovering on failure and still unprofitable until he opened a fifth store. He experienced setback after setback until he finally developed a formula that worked. Because DeLuca's original goal was to earn enough money to fund medical school, and because subsequent Subways sprung from a desire to make the original ones profitable, his first desire evolved into a new one. After he had opened sixteen locations, DeLuca turned to franchising for even greater growth. In other words, his first desire to fund medical school was transformed into a second and then a third desire.

Subway's growth was based on the KISS principle: "Keep it simple, stupid." Unlike other franchise systems, theirs offered easy entry and cost savings for franchisees for less expensive equipment, financing, supplies, and training. Even advertising was simplified into simple blockbuster ideas like "Seven subs under six grams of fat." The reason we love the Subway story is because the largest restaurant chain in the world would not have gotten off the ground had Fred DeLuca not had a burning desire to succeed, pushed through those early failures, and created an easily replicated business model that met an ongoing need.

Desire is *the* pre-requisite for success as an entrepreneur. It is what drives new business owners when they want to quit, empowers them with energy to keep going, and helps them persevere through tough times.

What about the person who can't perceive a specific desire? Believe it or not, there are ways to create desire when it is needed. How? From a technique known as autosuggestion. Napoleon Hill studied the lives of hundreds of successful Americans, and he discovered that high achievers first saw their goals in their mind's eye before achieving them. In Hill's view—channeling Edison—"the mind [can] produce anything the mind [can] conceive and believe."[5] Hill's research followed up on that of a pioneering French psychologist, Emile Coué, who published a book in 1920 titled *Self-Mastery through Conscious Autosuggestion.* Coué demonstrated that routine repetition of desired thoughts automatically changed a person's subconscious. Once the imagination desires a fixed outcome, the mindset begins to change. I had trouble believing something so simple could actually work, but I've found that it does. For years I looked at a photograph of a small insurance agency pasted in a "visualization book" and read a simple statement to myself twice a day: "I will build a commercial insurance agency specializing in casualty and write enough accounts to generate a premium of $5 million within five years." Did autosuggestion make a difference for me? Suffice it to say, I had a premium volume of $7 million in four years and I overachieved my goal of self-employment.

---

[5] Hill, *Think and Grow Rich*, 196.

Setting rewards for the accomplishment of specific goals can also generate desire, e.g., "Upon achievement of $5 million in premium volume, I will buy a new, luxury automobile." Such rewards can be powerful motivators.

A third method of generating desire is immersing yourself in a business specialty or trade. In my case, that specialty was commercial casualty insurance. I took courses for the Chartered Property Casualty Underwriter (CPCU) designation in casualty insurance, memorized the exclusions contained in the primary coverage policy, general liability, and modeled my practices after the leaders in the field. This emulating tactic generated a lot of desire. By watching the best insurance producers in my city and studying their ways and habits, I became familiar with what it took to succeed in the industry.

Finally, regardless of the source of your desire (innate or generated), make it a practice to remind yourself regularly of your dream. Build enthusiasm for your goals by reminding yourself of them on a daily basis. Envision your idea for self-employment, the rewards you will reap, and the feelings of happiness you will experience. It is the law of cause and effect. You send out the cause of the affirmation—your autosuggestion—and the effect eventually becomes manifest.

I started my first insurance agency in Jacksonville, Florida, which at the time was a medium-sized city with a small group of elite business leaders. My direct insurance company wrote automobile dealers at a competitive price. It turned out the first dealership I gained an opportunity to quote was Platt Pontiac, owned by a prominent Jacksonville businessman named Harry Platt. He was not only a successful dealer, but he had also married into the wealthy DuPont family. I remember one particular day as though it were yesterday. My insurance bid was handwritten on three sheets of paper though the coverage benefits and low premiums were well-displayed. After some give and take, Platt told me I had an order and to write-up the binder for coverage. I got into my used Oldsmobile for the return trip to my office, and I began the drive banging my steering wheel and screaming at the top of my lungs. I knew full well that his order was a major breakthrough. Not only was it the first of many dealerships as clients for my business, but I had also broken into a power elite. Only a fervent desire to succeed could have fueled such an outburst of joy and satisfaction.

As with any new undertaking you have to believe in yourself, in your ideas. Belief is the final piece of desire. If you want something, but you think it is impossible, you probably won't make it happen. You can't only manifest an idea for a new business by wanting it. You've got to believe in yourself and in your new venture. Your level of commitment stems from your ability to believe your objective can work. Desire and belief together cause a person to take action. Truly wanting something, wishing for it to happen, is the starting point to setting your own salary.

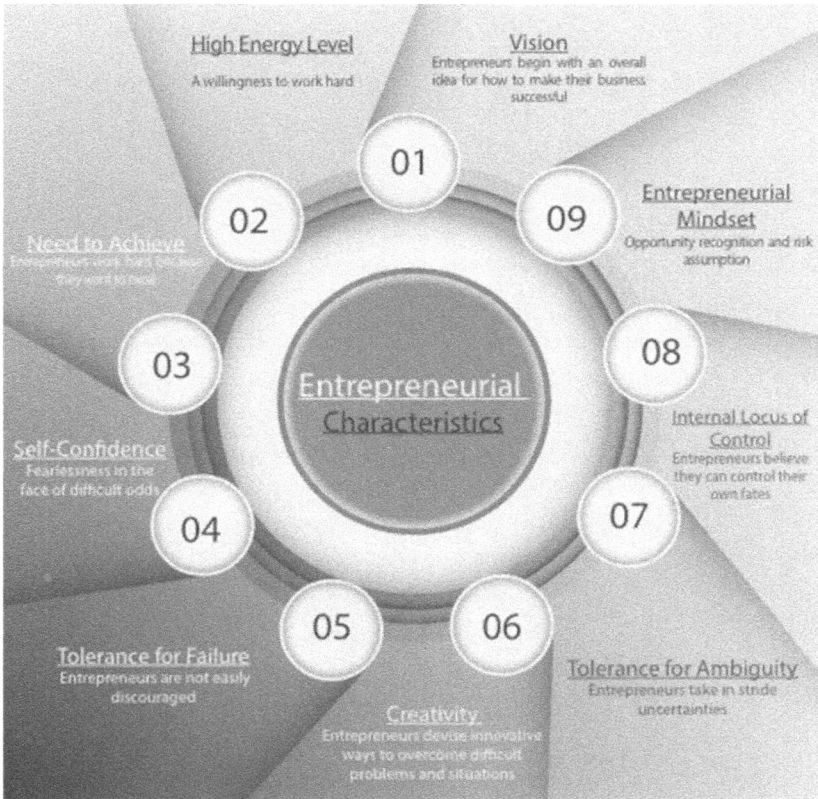

High Energy Level
A willingness to work hard

Vision
Entrepreneurs begin with an overall idea for how to make their business successful

01

02

09

Entrepreneurial Mindset
Opportunity recognition and risk assumption

Need to Achieve
Entrepreneurs work hard because they want to excel

03

08

Entrepreneurial Characteristics

Internal Locus of Control
Entrepreneurs believe they can control their own fates

Self-Confidence
Fearlessness in the face of difficult odds

04

07

05

06

Tolerance for Failure
Entrepreneurs are not easily discouraged

Creativity
Entrepreneurs devise innovative ways to overcome difficult problems and situations

Tolerance for Ambiguity
Entrepreneurs take in stride uncertainties

Takeaway from Chapter One

Generate a burning desire.

CHAPTER TWO

Send Out a Cause

Genius is the ability to put into effect what is on your mind.
— F. Scott Fitzgerald

As far back as Aristotle, philosophers have recognized the essential role of causation. This principle is so powerful it is referred to as "the iron law of human destiny." A law of cause and effect states that absolutely everything happens for a reason, and all actions have consequences. For every outcome or effect in anyone's life, there is a specific cause. Once the law is understood, the wonderful thing about it is we can create what we want by acting in a manner to bring about the desired result. Without realizing I was using this universal law, I put together my first insurance agency. I set in motion a chain of effects that led me to my first business success. Three or four of us young, eager agents decided there were three bibles, our so-called "magic books," to learn and shape a successful business future. They were Napoleon Hill's aforementioned book *Think and Grow Rich*, Dale Carnegie's *How to Win Friends and Influence People*, and *Psycho-Cybernetics* by Dr. Maxwell Maltz. For many years we lived with these books, consumed their contents, and tried to apply their principles. Guidelines from these books helped form a mindset of causations that directly impacted what was to come for us. From Napoleon Hill, I took away the importance of goal setting. From Dale Carnegie, I found the need to focus on other people's interests. And from Maxwell Maltz, I discovered the image of having already succeeded.

All of us are a product of our backgrounds and life experiences. I was fortunate enough to grow up in the home of a successful entrepreneur in northern California. My father, Curtis Day, specialized in insurance for building contractors, and he instilled an underlying confidence that self-employment was the best option and a value that defined success. In fact, his model was the first cause embedded in my character, which later was enhanced by the practices espoused in the three key books. Looking back, there was little doubt that at some point in my life I was going to try my own hand at starting a business. It could easily have been unsuccessful, and I might have fallen flat on my face, but from the earliest time I can remember, I was planning on following my father's example. The trouble was he cast a large shadow in downtown San Francisco, and I saw little chance to prove that my efforts would be mine alone.

With the support of my equally ambitious wife Donna, we plotted a bold plan to move to a completely new city, chosen for the potential of its demographics, adventure, and opportunity. Taking a day off from our jobs, we plotted our criteria and goals, ultimately choosing Jacksonville, Florida as our destination. Only Donna had actually visited the city once before, but it met our conditions: a population between 500,000 and one million people, a location in the Southeastern "Sun Belt," and the presence of numerous medical and insurance companies. Donna was a registered physical therapist and was able to easily transfer her license from California to Florida, but I was required to work for another insurance agent before I could become eligible for an insurance license in Florida.

What became the start of several entrepreneurial ventures unfolded in Jacksonville as a series of uncanny and synchronistic events that can only be attributed to the law of cause and effect. From my arrival in Florida onward, I focused on putting together a plan to start my own commercial, property, and casualty insurance agency. Besides a license, I needed a network, two or three trade specialties, and a competitive insurance product. The latter was what we sometimes call a "hot" market. Knowing what I wanted in my plan, I was subconsciously sending out the cause each and every day. After a year of working for a larger insurance broker specializing in the same kind of casualty accounts, my opportunity presented itself.

A set of circumstances started with what seemed like a series of coincidences. First, my boss, who wrote surety bonds, told me about a small, personal lines agent who had written a difficult bond across town with an unknown company named Cotton States. Next, I lost a quotation on a small rural electric cooperative in middle Georgia to a company called Cotton States, and finally, while attending my license preparation course in Orlando, fellow students were talking about a competitive, new insurance company by the name of Cotton States. Wanting to start my own agency, looking for a competitive product, and needing a strong backer, I drove straight to their home office on my next business trip to Atlanta. This chain of events was pure cause and effect. I was all eyes and ears, ready at all times for such an opportunity because I was sending out the cause for such an effect for a long time. I knew right away in my gut this company was divine providence, the perfect coming together of my goal at the right time.

Why was I prepared to receive this effect and pounce on Cotton States? It was because I had focused long before on the goal of my own insurance agency. I had affirmed my goal as an objective, and using autosuggestion I visualized an endpoint that placed me in a successful position. In essence, I was following the old adage: "Success is where opportunity and preparation meet." Thanks to my cause of preparation, my subconscious mind recognized Cotton States as my desired effect. Maxwell Maltz had given me self-confidence, Napoleon Hill had clarified my goals, and Dale Carnegie had sharpened my people skills. I used them all at the right time to arrange an agent appointment to start my business. I was ambitious, had the right experience, and was looking for an edge. While entrepreneurs share many common traits such as ambition, competitiveness, creativity, and persistence, none of them has all the same characteristics. Over time, research has shown only one characteristic is common to all entrepreneurs: a mindset that recognizes opportunity, combined with a willingness to take risks. Entrepreneurship is to see opportunity others do not.[6]

My experience with Cotton States had its complications. They were a direct writing insurance company, meaning they owned the policy expirations instead of me. Also, their commission scale was lower, and their focus was more on life rather than casualty coverage. I had to take a large risk, commit to a less financially stable carrier, and leave a good paying job

---

[6] G.E. Hills, R.C. Shrader, and G.T. Lumpkin, "Opportunity Recognition as a Creative Process," *Frontiers of Entrepreneurship Research*, (Babson College, Wellesley, MA), 1999.

with a national firm. Although I had to stick my neck out, all my instincts told me it was the opportunity I sought, and my many causes had snagged their desired effect. To take advantage of what I knew in my heart was right, I had to rent an office space, return the company car, buy office furniture, sign a restrictive contract, and cut ties with the large bureau companies to take advantage of the opportunity. I am certain I would not have been able to recognize this chance for what it was had I not been sending out the right causes of preparation, planning, and subconscious programming along the way.

The move wasn't an easy decision either. My wife and I walked along Jacksonville Beach for many hours trying to decide whether to take Cotton States' monthly draw for a lower commission scale or to take nothing and have a higher commission and rely on my wife's salary for monthly expenses. We look back today with a smile when we talk about the agony of our decision not to accept a lower commission scale in exchange for a monthly stipend from Cotton States. We chose to finance the startup business ourselves and take advantage of normal commission. Fortunately, victory is the child of preparation and determination, and my plan was a good one. Within six months we had collected three times more in cash payments than my previous annual salary. Our good timing allowed us to launch the first of three successful insurance agencies.

One of the reasons I was ready to take advantage of this opportunity was mentorship. My father served as an early example of a self-employed insurance broker specializing in a specific trade. He exposed me to effective underwriting and accounting practices that built a solid foundation for my future. Every aspiring entrepreneur should follow a similar path. Mentors fill gaps and help people grow by sharing their knowledge and providing advice and encouragement. A beginner should try to choose a mentor who is already successful in the field he or she wants to pursue. A mentor can be a boss or an acquaintance. When I ask my students to interview business owners, they consistently report a willingness on the part of entrepreneurs to share their stories. Almost without exception, successful people like to be asked about their experiences, want to share their knowledge, and are open to all manner of questions. To them it's a validation of their achievements.

It seems the more successful a person is, the easier they are to approach. This fact can be used to advantage by every person starting out.

Aspiring entrepreneurs have to know what they need in terms of mentorship. They need to be responsible and invest time in good relationships. The Small Business Administration (SBA) includes mentoring's importance to new ventures as one of its ten steps to "Starting a Business."[7]

Among the helpful organizations are SCORE (Senior Corps of Retired Executives) and SBDCs (Small Business Development Centers). Other resources are sponsored by state governments and women's, veterans', and minority business associations. A newcomer should work at establishing mutually beneficial but structured relationships. Structure means respecting a mentor's time, coming prepared to scheduled meetings, and using notes and action plans for follow-ups. Showing gratitude for their help is also an important aspect of a relationship. The mentor concept works only as long as the mentor feels his or her contributions are being appreciated. The greater the appreciation, the greater the benefit.

Key bosses along the way can likewise serve as important resources, because they can provide targeted information and advice. During my professional journey, I received two pieces of advice from mentors that saved my business at different points in my career. The advice involved the use of fiduciary accounts for company premiums and the idea of a silent joint venture for surety bonding. One mentor taught me to always segregate fiduciary premiums from agency funds, while the other exposed me to different ways to make a surety bond acceptable to an underwriter. After moving to Florida, I automatically put fiduciary premiums in a separate account although at the time this practice was not the rule. One day an officer of Cotton States visited unannounced and demanded a full accounting of past-due premiums that we had long withheld due to incorrect record keeping. I am certain I would have been terminated as an agent and put out of business had I not been able to write a six-figure check that day after reconciliation of the balance due. I was able to write that check only because the funds were safely parked in a separate account. The other

---

[7] Caron Beesley, "Why A Mentor Is Key to Small Business Growth and Survival," *SBA.gov,* 2014, https://www.sba.gov/blogs/why-mentor-key-small-business-growth-and-survival-0.

incident involved a performance bond for a large prison building in New York City. My contractor had spent over one million dollars at the time he requested the bond to get paid by the city. The request came unexpectedly and in an amount far exceeding earlier limits. While it took me three months to write the bond, it was made possible—and my agency saved from a major setback—by using a technique taught to me by a mentor called "silent joint venture." By joining my contractor into a subcontract with another contractor on the same project, two surety companies were able to underwrite an otherwise impossible bond. Knowledge of these practical business tips can only come from experience, either your own or borrowed from others like mentors.

Entrepreneurship as a Career

1 More than 11% of Americans run their own businesses.

2 In an average month, Americans start approximately 465,000 new businesses

3 The past two decades have shown a heightened interest in entrepreneurial careers.

4 People choose entrepreneurship for many reasons:
Dissatisfaction with traditional work
Their ideas fulfill customer needs

Takeaway from Chapter Two

The Law of Cause and Effect rules the world.

CHAPTER THREE

Generate Ideas

Everything you possess of skill, and wealth and handicraft,
wasn't it first merely a thought and a quest?

— *Rumi*
Thirteenth-century Persian Poet

In an August 2014 TED Talk, Nick Hanauer, a billionaire entrepreneur and early investor in over thirty companies, summed up the creation of entrepreneurial ideas very succinctly: "Intuition about the future is the essence of good entrepreneurship."[8]

With this in mind, it becomes a matter of what you are going to do, what you are going to invent, or what problem you are choosing to solve. Ideas come from many spaces: your past, your education, your experiences and hobbies. They also come from personal observation like changes in markets (think global), inventions (airplanes), competition (Subway vs. hamburger), and technology (smartphones). An idea can originate from happenstance, a serendipitous moment, an accidental breakthrough, or from a process of mental focus called "flow." Mihaly Csikszentmihalyi's work in psychology shows that when external conditions match our goals, the sense of mastery or positive feedback promotes creativity.[9] Flow, also known as "the zone," is the mental state in which a person is immersed in a feeling of energized focus of full involvement. When information comes

---

[8] Nick Hanauer, 2014, "Beware, Fellow Plutocrats, The Pitchforks Are Coming," Presentation, TEDSalon New York.
[9] Mihaly Csikszentmihalyi, *Creativity: The Psychology of Discovery and Invention,* (New York: Harper Perennial Modern Classics, 2013).

into awareness that is congruent with our goals, we undergo an optimal experience or a state of consciousness Csikszentmihalyi calls "flow."

Thomas Edison was in this flow when he worked in his lab at Menlo Park, New Jersey, creating the first practical light bulb, sound recording devices, motion picture machines, and the nickel-iron battery. His favorite pastimes were reading and experimenting (and undoubtedly day dreaming), and he was famous for sleeping just three to fours hours a night so that he had plenty of time to get into an innovative flow. His 3,500 notebooks have been preserved, and they reveal his brainstorms and a visual history of Edison's mind at work. As Michael Michalko writes, Edison's journals "show creative thinking depends on continuing the flow of ideas long enough to purge the common, habitual ones and produce the unusual and imaginative."[10]

Some of these ideas come from getting close to the customer, from focus groups, from library and Internet research, and from human-centered discovery. The latest methodology in entrepreneurship is called the Lean Startup, and its focal point on the *potential* customer. A Lean Startup begins with only the minimum of necessary resources and searches for a successful business model from a hypothesis or starting thought. It constantly checks with potential customers about the value of an idea, a product or a service. Customer feedback is used to adjust the idea by making "pivots," or revisions, until something the customers want or like is found. The Lean Startup method nearly puts idea generation on autopilot in the sense it relies on the potential customer to tell an entrepreneur what is needed for a "better mousetrap."

A modern way to come up with ideas, new products, or a new service method is to use *design thinking*. This process involves approaching an idea by fully defining it from many angles. In Silicon Valley there are firms that employ teams—the leading one is Ideo founded by David Kelley—of complementary members who collaborate on their innovations. One person might be good at engineering, another good at numbers, and still another at marketing. Working together creates a synergy, generating ideas

---

[10] Michael Michalko, "Thomas Edison's Creative Thinking Habits," *Creative Thinking*, 2013, http://creativethinking.net/thomas-edisons-creative-thinking-habits/#sthash.dJXZImcY.mI7GX5je.dpbs.

that are stronger than would result from individuals. For example, Steve Jobs set up a team at Apple that operated a separate lab away from the rest of the company. This group developed the McIntosh computer. Many Google employees are given one day of free time each week to imagine and innovate new ideas. This "free" time has produced innovations like Gmail, Google Transit, Google News and Google Talk. Likewise, it was a collaborative team at Lockheed during World War II that designed the famous P-80 turbojet-powered combat aircraft.

Dr. Bruce Barringer of the Oklahoma State University believes most successful new business ideas result from recognizing the ways value can be added to one of three sources: environmental trends (economic, social, technological, and regulatory changes), unsolved problems (which John W. Gardner calls "brilliantly disguised opportunities"), and gaps in the marketplace (plus-sized clothing). In lieu of a full lean startup, Barringer uses what he calls a "first screen," a shorter idea analysis which tests for strength (value), industry (growth), target customers (purchasing), founder (experience), and financial issues (capital), which results in an overall score for the potential business idea.

The story of the Dyson vacuum cleaner is a good example of a new business birthed by a value-adding idea. James Dyson is a British engineer whose determination was forged by his long-distance running. He became frustrated when dust kept clogging his vacuum cleaner, so he came up with the idea of "cyclone separation," preventing the loss of suction. What makes Dyson's story so incredible is that Dyson never stopped innovating. In 1983, after five years working on prototypes—supported by his wife's salary as a teacher—Dyson designed his G-Force cleaner, the first vacuum not to use a bag. Because his invention posed a threat to the lucrative replacement bag business, he was unable to find a manufacturer in the United Kingdom or the United States. Fortunately, he found a Japanese company willing to license his design and build the G-Force.

The G-Force initially relied on catalog sales. When Dyson's vacuum finally broke into the UK market in 1991, annual sales for disposable cleaner bags had topped at $140 million. Rather than explaining G-Force's suction technology, Dyson launched a successful advertising campaign emphasizing the slogan "Goodbye to the Bag." His dual cyclone vacuum cleaner became the fastest selling vacuum ever made. Dyson still loves to tinker and says he would rather work on the factory floor with the engineers than spend time managing his vast company. As a result, new devices and more improvements have continued over the years. For example, his latest vacuum is a lightweight cordless with a longer lasting battery and a smaller but more powerful motor. In addition, his hand dryer has been widely implemented for its functionality. The device is appropriately called the "Airblade," and you pull your hands through strong currents of warm air.

Henry J. Kaiser was another inspiring American entrepreneur who used a series of imaginative ideas to start an array of businesses in California. He is credited with coining the phrase "Find a need and fill it," a wonderful expression of entrepreneurship. Kaiser started a construction company, a cement company, a steel and aluminum company, a ship-building company, and a car company. He found a need and filled it when he discovered that his employees—his companies employed thousands of folks—needed health benefits. So Kaiser developed the United States' first large-scale, health maintenance organization (HMO) in 1945. After seventy years, Kaiser Permanente is now the largest managed care organization in the US.

Even when Henry Kaiser retired, he kept busy. He found an undeveloped spot on the Hawaiian island of Oahu to create his and many other retirees' Polynesian homes in a place named Hawaii Kai (for Kaiser of course). As a child growing up in the San Francisco Bay area, I remember the Kaiser concrete trucks painted a bright pink color and bearing the words "Find a Need and Fill It" on their doors. Concrete poured into the foundations of many high rises were not only filling construction needs but also metaphorically representing how Kaiser created new businesses. Each of his enterprises set the stage for his next venture.

A major aspect of idea creation spins off *opportunity recognition*. While entrepreneurial opportunities surround us every day, it takes a keen awareness of trends, needs, and events to recognize them. Experts call this "mindfulness," or "cognitive recognition," which is the process in our brains that notices, stores, retrieves, and processes information. Having a good memory helps. Expertise in the field of interest is also beneficial, because the more you know, the easier it is to generate new ideas within the industry. Hence, mentoring under another entrepreneur long enough to learn the field of interest increases opportunity recognition. My successful idea resulted from experience with commercial insurance.

An example of someone generating a better idea is Michael Bloomberg, the billionaire former Mayor of New York City. After completing his studies at Johns Hopkins and Harvard, he joined Salomon Brothers on Wall Street and immersed himself for fifteen years in the business of investment securities. Bloomberg quickly climbed the ladder, and when Salomon was bought in 1981, Bloomberg used his severance pay to start his own company. His insider status positioned him to see opportunities created by the emerging technological revolution and the shift toward digitization. His new company would deliver high-quality information in diverse formats to the investment community on a much faster platform. Bloomberg's first customer was Merrill Lynch. They invested $30 million in what was then called Innovative Market Systems, now Bloomberg, LLP. By 1990, his data and media company had installed eight thousand "Market Master" terminals at the desks of traders. By 2012, they had 310,000 terminals worldwide. Ancillary products were then added such as *Bloomberg News*, Bloomberg Message, and Bloomberg Tradebook. In 2012, *Forbes* put his wealth at $33 billion and ranked him the thirteenth richest person in the world. Bloomberg's opportunity recognition was seeing a need for better financial data and putting it together in a new format with speedier distribution and better content but only after his years of observation working inside his specialty field.

Shahid Khan, current owner of the NFL Jacksonville Jaguars, is a Pakistani immigrant who came to the US at age sixteen to study engineering at the University of Illinois, Urbana-Champaign. His first job was washing dishes. From there he worked part-time for the automotive manufacturing company Flex-N-Gate while studying engineering. Upon graduation, he went to work full-time as their director of engineering. Seven years later he started Bumper Works, a niche bumper manufacturer that sold pickup truck and body shop replacement bumpers. After another three years, Khan purchased his old employer, Flex-N-Gate, and greatly expanded operations to include the big three automakers. Khan's years of experience— first as an employee, then as an entrepreneur—enabled him to "connect the dots" already stored in memory. This "cognitive recognition process" led him to perceive the potential, added value of acquiring Flex-N-Gate, and manufacturing a single assembly bumper inside a limited window of opportunity.

Ideas do not have to be virgin new. An entrepreneur can redesign an existing service, customize a popular product, or simply invent a better way of doing business. One of the best ways to become an entrepreneur is to be, in effect, a copycat. Take a popular, successful business and copy its winning formula. Look no further than the fast food business for proof of how a large market can make room for another provider with a different method of providing the same product.

Chick-fil-A started as a small restaurant which catered to Ford Motor Co. employees in a suburb of Atlanta, Georgia. Its culture has been heavily influenced by founder S. Truett Cathy, a devout Baptist whose work ethic is legendary. Chick-fil-A now has over 1,850 restaurants in forty-one states and to this day is still closed on Sundays. Cathy reinvented fast food by focusing on the chicken sandwich as his company's core product, and then he formed a new chain restaurant model by retaining ownership of each location. The company sets up operators instead of franchisees, thereby keeping a larger percentage of sales. Their national advertising campaigns are unique as well, featuring cows who selfishly suggest people should "Eat Mor Chikin" to save their hides. Those of us who live in the Southeast can attest to the popularity of Chick-fil-A. It has invented an incredibly successful formula that is so popular that its restaurants are packed with patrons. Its annual sales now exceed $5 billion. Chick-fil-A's success demonstrates how there is always room for a new, better way of doing something already in demand and desired by the buying public.

Ideas for new services can be just as powerful as product-related ideas. One such example resulted from an undergraduate project. Fred Smith, a fellow Vietnam veteran, sensed the need for a rapid delivery service in the days before the Internet in a paper-laden world. His idea was for a bank-like clearinghouse for overnight, airfreight operations. It would be located in the geographic middle of its regional centers. Fred Smith's story and that of Federal Express is legendary. While an undergraduate at Yale, Smith wrote a term paper on how existing routes used by airfreight shippers were economically inadequate. He noticed the great difficulty in getting packages delivered within one or two days. After completion of his military service, Smith bought controlling interest in a Little Rock, Arkansas aviation company, using a $4 million inheritance. He then did nationwide research into improving the inefficient airfreight distribution system, and his solution revolutionized global business, setting the standard for speed and reliability. In the company's early days, Smith went to great lengths to keep his operation afloat. He once took the company's last $5,000 to Las Vegas—or so the legend goes—and won $27,000 playing blackjack to cover a $24,000 fuel bill. Today, FedEx is headquartered in Memphis, Tennessee and has annual revenues of $45 billion. The company employs more than 300,000 people and is ranked among the most admired employers in the country.

What do these diverse startups all have in common? They are examples of better ideas that meet large-scale needs. Entrepreneurs create value by giving customers what they want, sometimes before they even know it. Dyson's vacuum cleaner eliminated the dust bag, Kaiser's industrial acumen helped win a war, Bloomberg reengineered the delivery of financial news, Khan consolidated car parts production, Cathy's chicken introduced a new taste, and Smith's overnight shipments shrunk the world. These entrepreneurs succeeded because they brought improved solutions to market segments. They built sustainable advantages over competitors, differentiated products through innovations, and added value for their customers. What is striking about this group of individuals is that none of them were overnight successes. All put in apprenticeships, learned their crafts while working elsewhere first, and found their opportunities while working *inside* their industries. Even the so-called quick billionaires who pioneered the digital revolution paid their dues. Bill Gates started at age fourteen spending extra time in his school's computer lab, Steve Jobs worked a night shift at Atari games, and Dave Packard learned electronics at General Electric's manufacturing plants. In all of these examples, the inspiration for their ideas was rooted in trial and error and work experience, and they forever transformed the world.

Generate Ideas:

1. Consider your own experience, education, interests, and hobbies.
2. Use personal observations, (market changes, internet needs, competition profile, and inventions).
3. What can you invent, what problem can you solve or improve?
4. Put awareness in alignment with goals (like Edison did).
5. Get close to the customer (their needs, wants, and problems through "Creaction" and lean startup).
6. Use focus groups and design thinking (like Ideao and Google).
7. Be ready to pay your dues (Jobs = Atari, Gates = HS computer lab, David Packard = General Electric).
8. Innovate a better idea that appeals to a large need.

Takeaway from Chapter Three

Build a better mousetrap
and the world will beat a path to your door.

CHAPTER FOUR

Think Outside the Box

No, no, you're not thinking; you're just being logical.
– Niels Bohr
Nobel Laureate, Physics

How exactly do you get your mind outside the box and design that better mousetrap? This is a critical question to answer because it lies at the heart of entrepreneurship. John Steinbeck is credited with saying, "Ideas are like rabbits. You get a couple and learn how to handle them, and pretty soon you have a dozen." It is difficult, however, to come up with ideas that are genuinely different. An aspiring entrepreneur has to push aside conventional boundaries, take a 360-degree tour around a topic, and hopefully develop a flash of insight. Thomas Kuhn called this process a "paradigm shift" in which one conceptual worldview is replaced with another. Successful entrepreneurship uses this fresh perspective to carve out a niche in a target market that will disrupt and replace current providers. The world of commerce is way too big to crack any other way. Above all, there has to be differentiation, a distinctive product or service that separates itself from the thundering herd; otherwise, it is simply too difficult to compete in a dog-eat-dog environment full of large, established companies.

Coming up with a unique product or service is a tall order, but that's precisely why it's such a predictor for success. As discussed in Chapter Three, there are many ways to generate ideas, but a winning one has to be unique and arouse in consumers an eager want (aforementioned Dale Carnegie). By thinking unconventionally or outside the box, a potential entrepreneur has a chance to brainstorm a product or service that could undercut or even eliminate competition.

Some ideas are so revolutionary they don't have competition. The telephone had the telegraph as competition, but its superiority quickly eliminated everything else. The same thing happened with the transistor that replaced vacuum tubes and eventually led to the microchip and modern computers. What makes an idea a blockbuster is its ability to promote growth. How far outside the box did the earlier designers have to think to envision an iPod for digital music, the iPad for tablet computing, or to stretch even further, an iPhone for a computer cellphone?

Paradigm shifting innovation is a prerequisite for sustainable growth. Breakthrough ideas can come in every field of commerce. Interestingly, consumer goods and automotive supplies actually outpace electronics in new products. Of course, radically new ideas are rare, but creative and incremental ways to improve existing products and services are being made every day. My recommendation is to focus on a field of interest, saturate yourself in that universe, and look for an edge in how to enhance what is currently being done. You'll have a much better chance of innovating an improvement or a better mousetrap by zeroing in on one area of the economy, especially a segment that generates plenty of revenue and has a large, established demand.

Elon Musk is a present day entrepreneur who is consistently a divergent thinker. As one of the founding partners at PayPal, Musk bypassed other Internet banking activities and focused on the potential of a money transfer service. PayPal became hugely successful because it provided a more efficient way to make payments online. It also became the first dot-com initial public offering (IPO) and was sold to eBay for $1.5 billion.

Musk, a South African from Pretoria, taught himself computer code in order to play a video game at age twelve. After earning a bachelor's degree from the University of Pennsylvania's Wharton School, Musk moved to California to work on a PhD at Stanford, but he quickly left to put his (outside the box) ideas into action. First, he and his brother started a software company called Zip2 that published city guides for major newspapers. It was sold to Compaq. Next came PayPal, followed quickly by SpaceX, which develops and manufactures space launch vehicles. In 2009, SpaceX's Falcon rocket became the first privately funded vehicle to put a satellite into earth orbit. Shortly after starting SpaceX, Musk invested in the electric car company Tesla Motors and, after the 2008 financial crisis, assumed leadership as CEO and product designer. Originally a sports car, Tesla is named after Nikola Tesla, the discoverer of AC current who was a contemporary of Thomas Edison. Musk introduced Tesla's four-door Model S in 2012 and has plans for a more affordable car to increase sales in 2016. His visionary concepts now include a new battery factory outside Reno, Nevada and a network of supercharging stations across North America. Musk thinks so outside the box he has raised a high bar. So far he has brought us PayPal, Telsa Motors, SpaceX, Solar City, and is working on a high-speed transportation system called Hyperloop.

Although he is worth $12 billion, Musk works a hundred hours a week. In a published interview, he reinforced the value of unconventional thinking. He said, "I don't believe in process," and "The problem is that at a lot of big companies, process becomes a substitute for thinking. You're encouraged to behave like a little gear in a complex machine."[11] As far as starting a company, he says, "You encounter issues you didn't expect, step on landmines. It's bad. Years two to four or five are usually quite difficult. A friend has a saying, 'It's eating glass and staring into the abyss.' There's a tremendous bias against taking risks. Everyone is trying to optimize their ass-covering . . . I think it's very important to have a feedback loop."[12]

In Chapter Two, I related the story of my first insurance agency and how I was sending out a cause. I was looking for a way to do something different in property and casualty production for small- to medium-sized businesses. At that point in life, I had no idea about thinking outside the box, but I did understand goal setting and believed in autosuggestion. I was telling myself regularly to find a means that would allow me to go into the insurance agency business. My training had been with large companies (the so-called Insurance Service Office or ISO bureau form) and independent insurance brokerage. These types of middlemen represent all insurance companies, and they are free to place their coverage with whichever company best suits an individual account. These agents had the freedom to leave one

---

[11] Chris Anderson, "Elon Musk's Mission to Mars," *Wired,* 2012,
http://www.wired.com/2012/10/ff-elon-musk-qa/.
[12] Ibid.

insurer and move to another if necessary. When Cotton States insurance came across my radar screen, I knew right away it was my opportunity, but their business model was new to me. Cotton States operated as a regional, direct writing insurance carrier, meaning they owned the policies, did not allow an agent to represent other companies, and priced both their policies and commissions differently.

What the differences meant was I had to stick my neck out, make a commitment to the unknown, and take a big risk on the future. In exchange for a more competitive premium (product), I received lower than normal commissions and had only one resource for coverage. My gut told me this new business model was the differentiation I needed to take on the competition, write a bunch of new accounts, and build a commercial insurance agency. My hunch proved to be right. I was able to write as many auto dealers, service subcontractors, and rural electric cooperatives—my three trade specialties—as I could physically get to and quote. I was a single producer soliciting accounts in a city I had moved to only a year before, and it would have been prohibitive to attempt a startup using the same insurance model as the other agents. The only reason I quickly established myself, "closed" orders for insurance, and eventually thrived was I had a viable, dynamically differentiated business plan based on a model for insurance out of the mainstream. I had successfully thought outside the conventional boundaries, gambled, and won.

On a larger scale, an example of thinking outside the box with a different business model is the story of Michael Dell. In the early days of personal computers, all non-Apple, desktop computers were manufactured, stocked as retail, and sold in stores. Back in those days the brands were Hewlett-Packard, Compaq, and Texas Instruments, among others. Dell, a native of Houston, Texas, began playing with computers at the age of twelve. While a freshman at the University of Texas, he started a small business putting together kits and selling upgrades for personal computers. He tried bidding on State of Texas business, and without the overhead of a retail store, began to win state contracts as a hardware supplier. Dell could see the potential for a manufacturer to save costs by selling PCs directly to consumers. From upgraded computers, kit sales, and add-on components in 1984, Dell evolved into a new PC business model, the build-on-demand personal computer.

By age twenty-seven in 1992, he was the youngest CEO of a Fortune 500 company, and in 2001 Dell became the largest personal computer maker. Michael Dell is a billionaire, and his company has offices in thirty-four countries with an employee workforce of 35,000. It was his thinking outside the conventional boundaries and then reinventing a new kind of delivery system for PCs—not making them until they were ordered—that brought the world to his doorstep. As Michael Dell explains, "It's through curiosity and looking at opportunities in new ways that we've always mapped our path at Dell. There's always an opportunity to make a difference. You don't have to be a genius or a visionary or even a college graduate to be successful. You just need a framework and a dream."[13]

Look around you, and try to think how the present ways of doing things might be improved. Entrepreneurs identify, evaluate, and develop their opportunities, which, in turn, are influenced by their experiences, education, immersions, and imagination. They are the individuals who visualize what they would like to accomplish and imagine their success. Breaking free from concepts and restraints, they think disruptively.

Michael Dell had tinkered since he was kid inside the workings of a personal computer. His success echoes the experience of Steve Jobs who had been an Altair 8800 hobbyist and my own experience working inside the property and casualty industry for five years. The three of us acquired enough knowledge to see beyond the accepted practices, recognize an opportunity, and take a risk to fill market demand in a new way.

Takeaway from Chapter Four

Entrepreneurial thinking doesn't begin with planning; it begins with a journey into your imagination.

---

[13] Michael S. Dell, "2003 University of Texas at Austin Commencement Address," Speech, 2003, University of Texas at Austin.

CHAPTER FIVE

What Kind of Business Should I Choose?

There are three constants in life . . . change, choice, and principles."

— *Stephen Covey*
Author of The 7 Habits of Highly Effective People

There are many ways to become an entrepreneur. If you long to be self-employed, own a business and set your own salary, the good news is you can do it. Be realistic, however, in your expectations. When people read about digital billionaires who have created revolutionary, world-changing products, they think that's entrepreneurship. To the contrary, most small business owners in the US are more aptly considered the dependable workhorses of our economy. They are the thousands of proprietors who labor tirelessly and power most of our economy by providing needed products and services. The plumber, the baker, and the gardener exemplify such entrepreneurs. An electrician, for example, can learn his trade working for a master and then buy his own truck and strike out for himself. By following the recommended guidelines outlined in this book, you can take some of the risks out of this process and join the ranks of the successful self-employed.

A few years back Thomas Stanley wrote the bestselling *The Millionaire Next Door*, defining who the rich in this country were and what they did. He came up with common rules and found many millionaires were self-employed, e.g., medicine, small manufacturing, and storefront retail. He learned that people who look rich actually might not be rich. Rather, they tend to overspend and have modest portfolios with lots of debt. The real millionaires tend to reside in middle-income neighborhoods, drive cars three to four years old, and live within their means. Stanley found that time is money in the sense that millionaires consciously set goals and take twice as much time planning budgets. His millionaires were happier living beneath their means partly because of the joy of being financially independent. His next-door millionaires were among those who could see the value of a specific market segment. Creating a unique company profile is important because entrepreneurs cannot be all things to all people, and finding the right niche is what enables a small business to exploit a competitive advantage.

Job satisfaction is a critical factor. Stanley's millionaires chose their occupations for more than the income. In *The Millionaire Next Door*, one millionaire explains, "The successful man is a guy who works at a job, who likes his work, who can't wait to get up in the morning to get down to the office."[14] The people Stanley studied lived below their means, chose their spouses carefully, and structured their daily lives. Other people "rented their lifestyle," so to speak, while the prudent "millionaires-to-be" lived simply, gradually building their net worth. As Peter Henry, Dean of New York University's Stern School of Business, explained, an individual's ability to delay gratification at a young age is a power predictor of future academic and professional achievement. In sum, the journey of entrepreneurship requires a little bit of risk and a whole lot of sacrifice upfront, but it can be ever so rewarding.

That said, here are some of the ways to consider a business for yourself using time-tested business models:

- ❖ **Franchising** – McDonald's, Subway, UPS store, etc. One party grants another party the right to use a trademark.
- ❖ **Middleman** – real estate agent, manufacturer's rep, wholesale broker, etc. Acts as a legal representative of a

---

[14] Thomas J. Stanley and William D. Danko, *The Millionaire Next Door: The Surprising Secrets of America's Wealthy*, (New York: Pocket Books, 1998), 240.

buyer or a seller helping sell a product or service to the consumer.

❖ **International trade** – Pier One, Toyota, Caterpillar, etc. These are financial transactions of global trade under which commodities of goods and services are sold to a foreign country. This category has exploded with growth in recent years because of the Internet.

❖ **Licensing** – license a technology à la Jim Dyson who licensed his vacuum cleaner in Japan to raise capital. This requires an intellectual property (patent, copyright, etc.).

❖ **Acquisition** – buy an existing company with on-going sales. Google bought YouTube. You should first consult with business brokers who buy and sell companies.

❖ **Startup** – a new venture from scratch. This can be based on an existing business model such as the plumber going out on his own or a brand new idea using Lean Startup methodology to create a new business model, e.g. FedEx.

❖ **A better mousetrap** – build a better mousetrap by redefining a product or service. Dyson's vacuum cleaner joined a crowded field but was simply better. (By the way, the U.S. Patent Office has actually issued 4,400 patents for better versions of the mousetrap.) They say research is to see what everybody else has seen and to think what nobody else has thought. For example, just when everyone thought there was no more room for another fast food restaurant serving hamburgers, Five Guys arrived. They sell the same product but have an especially juicy burger on a fresh bun along with perfect French fries. Started in Washington, D.C., Five Guys could not match McDonald's massive economies of scale (36,000 restaurants worldwide), but they could fill a premium burger niche in a target market.

A necessary ingredient to make any of these ownership choices is planning. The details of planning will be discussed in later chapters, but suffice it to say now that chances for entrepreneurial success depend in large measure on having a blueprint to follow. A new business venture can be compared to an orchestra filled with instruments, dependent on sheet music, but only as good as the conductor. Without the good idea, the motivation of desire, a good startup team, sufficient capital, and the support of other people, it's unlikely a new business will get off the ground. In my own example, I grew up in the house of a middleman, a person who transacted commercial insurance on behalf of clients to insurance carriers. My father started in the midst of the Great Depression in partnership with a fellow surety company employee who quit to start his own brokerage. They struggled to stay in business until World War II brought a boom in construction, and they wrote so many contract bonds on projects connected with war projects (including the Alcan Highway) their business flourished.

My father and I could be described as traditional entrepreneurs who embraced a proven method for starting a business as part of the normal flow of commerce. We both served as middlemen, providing access for our small business clients to the right combination of commercial, property, and casualty insurance coverage. What made our particular middlemen roles so lucrative was our built-in, repeat customer feature. Unlike life insurance policies, property and casualty policies are renewed on an annual basis. In addition, state law requires workers' compensation protecting employees from injury on the job and auto liability as a pre-requisite to licensing as part of the coverage package, meaning these things are a necessity to stay in business. Each year the coverage renews, and if agents minded their knitting, they had a good chance of renewing client coverage for another year. I can still hear my father calling the automatic renewal feature "one of the last, undiscovered legal rackets."

Because my father and I both replicated our companies and created other small business startups, we were called "serial entrepreneurs." There are also lifestyle entrepreneurs or those who set up their businesses to suit their way of life. My niece, a self-employed CPA in California, is a case in point. She worked from her home in public accounting for housing authorities that have strict federal accounting standards and requirements. After her two daughters were born and reached school age, she adjusted her bidding, workload, and schedule to suit her needs as a mother, and her business volume ebbed and flowed.

The most recent category of entrepreneurship is the virtual entrepreneur. Because of the Internet's global reach and the widespread acceptance of computer applications, one or two persons operating from a basement can develop a superior website business. Two former Yahoo! employees named Jan Koum and Brian Acton became disillusioned with the way Internet companies were fixated on advertising profits. They wanted to offer an advertising-free way for people anywhere in the world to text message without needing a service provider. Demand was so strong, particularly in third world countries that their new service, WhatsApp, caught on right away. And to Facebook it was both a potential goldmine and a serious competitor that represented the next billion users on the Internet. For these reasons, Facebook bought WhatsApp for $19 billion, which for Koum, a kid raised in a home on food stamps, was less important than helping disadvantaged people have an ability to text message.

Entrepreneurial Business Models:

1. Franchising
2. Middleman
3. International Trade
4. Licensing
5. Acquisition
6. Startup
7. Better Mousetrap

Takeaway from Chapter Five

If you want to have your own business, there is a way to do it.

CHAPTER SIX

The High Percentage Model

The first principle is that you must not fool yourself—and you are the easiest person to fool.

— *Richard Feynman*
Theoretical Physicist

After reading about all the entrepreneurial possibilities in Chapter Five, you may be feeling somewhat overwhelmed. Which way should I go? What are my strengths and weaknesses? Can I afford to leave my current job? Over the years, many of my students have expressed these same concerns, so I offer a model for self-employment with a better than average chance for success. I call it the "High Percentage Model" or HPM, and its purpose is to expedite your decision making and increase your odds for success based on past performance. Here are the parameters for the HPM:

1. **Choose a service business vs. a product business –** Service companies have a higher percentage of success. Our economy is 80 percent service-based which means there are more opportunities for a service idea than for a product idea as a new business venture. Moreover, Harris Interactive, a well-known market research company, conducted a customer survey, which determined that 88 percent of consumers preferred dealing with a company with strong customer service than one with the most innovative products. Another study found that 70 percent of customers leave one business for another because of poor customer

service. Not only is customer service more important than a product, but service companies also have a better chance for success. We live in a service economy. The current list of Fortune 500 companies contains more service companies and fewer manufacturers than ever before. The knowledge economy has only accelerated this trend. Growth of a business model called the product-service system (PSS) has created new ways for value creation by increasing the service component of any product.

In general, service-oriented businesses are easier to start, because there are no inventories or physical resources necessitating lots of capital. An entrepreneur can literally start a service company in his or her home with a card table and a smartphone versus the expenses of retail space, product, and labor. Service marketing expands the range of possibilities exponentially to a wide array of industries such as telecommunications, finance, hospitality, transportation, janitorial, and healthcare. Competitive advantage can be achieved easier in a service business because it is directly related to "inspiration and perspiration" (personal desire and effort). Entrepreneurs willing to work harder than competitors can attract customers and grow a business simply by providing a better service (cheaper, quicker, greater convenience) than others doing the same thing. Witness the success of entrepreneurs who are willing to work 24/7 in almost any business in fields like lodging, landscaping, and home healthcare. Satisfying customer needs or wants is what a service system provides, and the value proposition hinges on the customer's perception of how well those needs or wants are delivered. Provide better, quicker, and friendlier service, and customers will gravitate to your company.

2. **Use one or more types of bootstrapping** – Don't give up equity interest for capital in the initial phase and avoid applying for a standard business loan. Instead, tap your own resources for startup capital. Bootstrapping can reduce

risk by keeping debt manageable. It is the most common source of beginning stage funding because of its ease, control, and cost. Often, loans or advances out of personal savings or from friends or family are interest free and contain more flexible terms for repayment. Creative financing can also include crowdfunding, trade credit (more favorable terms by suppliers), factoring (sale of accounts receivables), and customer help (provision for a letter of credit, use of their equipment), and the leasing rather than purchase of real estate. Another means of bootstrapping is to minimize expenses by deferring personal compensation, working from home, renting equipment, and hiring temporary vs. permanent employees. Because no equity position has been relinquished and/or money formally borrowed, the business is worth more.

Bootstrapping is limited only by the entrepreneur's imagination. Money can come from retirement plans, asset sales, bartering, credit card advances, donations, and life insurance redemption. A good example of using bootstrap financing is a company named Aisle Planner whose developers sold everything they owned on Craigslist to fund their startup. *Inc.* Magazine's website recently named Aisle Planner as one of the top five wedding planning apps: "a cloud-based solution targeted to wedplanners, enabling them to more efficiently organize events and collaborate with clients, vendors and venues in a streamlined, time saving manner."[15]

Despite the obvious advantages of bootstrapping, some entrepreneurs may still seek equity funding. Certain factors such as high manufacturing costs or expensive equipment purchases could necessitate a large amount of money for the initial stage. At the very least, these startup

---

[15] Newlands, Murray, "Top 5 Wed-Apps Pivoting the Huge Wedding Industry," *Inc.,* 2014, http://www.inc.com/murray-newlands/top-5-wed-apps-pivoting-the-300b-wedding-industry.html.

entrepreneurs should be aware that when you seek funds from venture capitalists or angel investors, you give up a significant percentage of ownership to secure their funding. These investors are a very savvy group who know how to make money, and they usually do it at other people's expense. If equity financing is the route chosen, don't give up control of your company—i.e., never hand over more than forty-nine percent equity ownership to others. Once outside investors gain fifty or more percent, your control ends. Always fully explore self-funded options before considering equity funding.

3. **Redefine an existing service or create a new target segment –** Fred Smith redefined delivery when he began his FedEx overnight service. The WhatsApp geeks took text messaging from the developed world to a new target of third world countries. Use disruptive innovation to change a known service for the better. Discount department stores, online bookselling, and low-price, point-to-point airlines are examples of improving existing services to attract customers. Banking innovated 24-hour automated tellers, and Kresge introduced discount retail in the 1960s, renaming itself K-Mart. Another way to build a new business is to scale a niche into a mass market. Christensen and Raynor, authors of *The Innovator's Solution: Creating and Sustaining Successful Growth,*" cite Black & Decker power tools, Canon copiers, and Honda motorcycles as examples of products scaled larger and now sold worldwide.[16]

Startups are agile and a new target segment can be created through a remix of the four P's of marketing: *product, place, price,* and *promotion.* Refine a niche service (product) wanted by a narrow segment, such as Hampton Inn and the business traveler. Price a service according to the budget of the target, and you'll create new value.

---

[16] Christensen, Clayton M., and Michael E. Raynor, *The Innovator's Solution: Creating and Sustaining Successful Growth,* (Boston, MA: Harvard Business Review Press 2013).

Choose the right kind of promotion (advertising, direct marketing, personal selling) to reach the specific target segment, or focus on the appropriate place/location to position the product for your target. For example, placing hotels off interstate highways in the case of Hampton Inns.

4. **Solve an existing, chronic customer complaint** – Often, all a new entrepreneur needs to do is look around. Opportunity recognition is one of the two entrepreneurship foundations (the other being risk assumption), and opportunity frequently becomes apparent due to consumer frustration. For example, hotel swipe cards solved the problem of guests losing keys to hotel rooms by enabling quick duplication and the subsequent elimination of front desk keys. Sara Blakely solved complaints about women's pantyhose by creating blemish free undergarments. Using a pair of scissors, she cut the feet off her control top pantyhose, solved a major complaint by women, filled the need of consumers, and started the Spanx revolution that made her a billionaire.

Brainstorming is done through creative problem solving. Begin by defining the problem precisely in specific terms. Next, gather all related facts and set any barriers aside. Be willing to accept divergent ideas from team members. Finally, visualize solutions and remember to stay flexible throughout. Record good and bad points for each solution idea, and then select and strengthen solutions. One technique is called the decision tree, which is a diagram that reflects all the possible choices and related outcomes. Branches of the tree are mutually exclusive, and a decision to use one choice can generate the need for many subchoices.

Once a target industry is chosen, a deep dive into its specific customer base can identify problems in need of solutions. The North American Industry Classification Systems (NAICS) can be used to collect and analyze data from the *census.gov* website. If a source already has significant knowledge about a specific industry, it can serve as a valuable knowledge base from which to solve problems. For example, as a commercial insurance agent for five years, I saw several opportunities before I chose one in particular for a new venture. Only from the inside can an observer see customer needs and areas of dissatisfaction clearly and then the opportunity for improvement in the form of a better service (Netflix vs. Blockbuster).

5. **Iterate with target customers to find an unmet need –** This technique relies on a systematic survey of potential customer wants and needs and is one of the pillars of Lean Startup methodology. Steve Blank, a successful author and serial entrepreneur, is credited with inspiring the Lean Startup movement, which is based on highly focused customer research. It involves testing hypotheses and "pivoting" (making a large change) or "iterating" (recalculating after a minor change) until a successful model is found. By the time customers fully articulate what they want, enough is known to sustain a larger commitment in both money and time. Most recently created web-based companies have used this method to fine-tune customer needs (think robotics, 3M surgical drapes, ergonomic toothbrushes). As Blank explains it, the Lean Startup process has three elements: 1) a Business Model Canvas to frame hypotheses, 2) customer development to test these hypotheses, and 3) the capability to build a succession of minimum viable products.

A Swiss business consultant named Alexander Osterwalder first developed the Business Model Canvas (BMC). It is a strategic management and entrepreneurial tool that allows design of a business using nine sections (see illustration on the next page).

BUSINESS MODEL CANVAS BY OSTERWALDER

KEY PARTNERS	KEY ACTIVITIES	VALUE PROPOSITIONS	CUSTOMER RELATIONSHIPS	CUSTOMER SEGMENTS
Who are our key partners? Who are our key suppliers? Which key resources are we acquiring from our partners? Which key activities do partners perform?	What key activities do our value propositions require? Our distribution channels? Customer relationships? Revenue streams?	What value do we deliver to the customer? Which one of our customers' problems are we helping to solve? What bundles of products and services are we offering to each segment? Which customer needs are we satisfying? What is the minimum viable product?	How do we get, keep, and grow customers? Which customer relationships have we established? How are they integrated with the rest of our business model? How costly are they?	For whom are we creating value? Who are our most important customers? What are the customer archetypes?

KEY RESOURCES

What key resources do our value propositions require? Our distribution channels? Customer relationships? Revenue streams?

CHANNELS

Through which channels do our customer segments want to be reached? How do other companies reach them now? Which ones work best? Which ones are most cost-efficient? How are we integrating them with customer routines?

COST STRUCTURE

What are the most important costs inherent to our business model? Which key resources are most expensive? Which key activities are most expensive?

REVENUE STREAMS

For what value are our customers really willing to pay? For what do they currently pay? What is the revenue model? What are the pricing tactics?

Osterwalder's canvas adapts the traditional business plan, which is essentially a document about what you plan to do and how to do it. The BMC contains nine building blocks for design activity—key partners, key activities, key resources, value propositions, customer relationships, (marketing) channels, customer segments, cost structure, and revenue streams. Planning is then organized into these niche segments, and the designer's thinking focuses on the key components of a new venture. Osterwalder developed a related methodology, called the Value Proposition Canvas, and Blank has been quick to acknowledge its importance and connection to the Lean Startup process. Essentially, Osterwalder focuses on the relationship between the Value Proposition (new product or service) and the Customer Segment. In combination, they become the all-important "Product-Market Fit," which is the sweet spot for entrepreneurs (see illustration).

Product-Market Fit

The Product-Market Fit is the degree to which a product satisfies a strong market demand to allow the expenditure of capital to scale a company.

Value Proposition

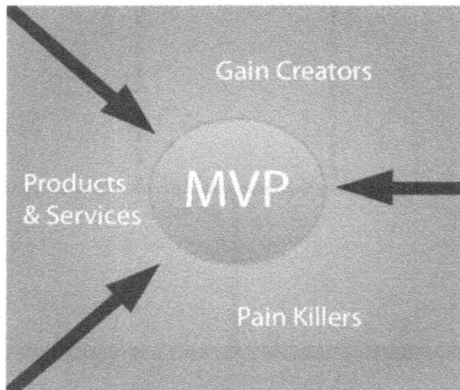

Customer Segment

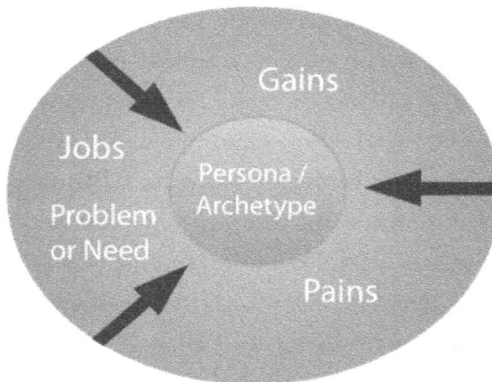

This expression of the Product-Market Fit by Steve Blank is drawn from the Business Model Canvas on page 39.

The Lean Startup is the best method to increase an aspiring entrepreneur's chances for success because it comprehensively tests marketing early on as opposed to perfecting the product or service model before going to market. In the absence of a known idea for a service or product, the new entrepreneur can use Lean Startup to discover an unmet need and design a new service or product to satisfy it. A target industry can be reverse engineered (i.e., perform a detailed survey of wants and needs using the customer development method to find a new way of doing things and design a new product). In the process of validating a real demand, a new service might be discovered, and the target audience might shift as well. Chapter Seven will discuss the basis for the Lean Startup method in more detail.

A good Lean Startup example is a company named d.light. In 2006, two MBA students set out to address the needs of millions of consumers in developing countries who lack access to reliable electricity. As a Peace Corps volunteer in the Republic of Benin in Africa in 2004, Sam Goldman witnessed his neighbor being badly burned by an overturned kerosene lantern, the standard source for home lighting. Goldman and his co-founder, Ned Tozun, took an Entrepreneurial Design for Affordability course at Stanford University, and over a three-year period, they developed a series of prototypes that led to an inexpensive solar lantern that could be mass produced. They readily attribute their success to this class, nicknamed "Touchy Feely," because it emphasized interactions between people and cultures. Today, d.light has sold over 8 million solar light and power products in sixty-two countries, thereby saving families $275 million a year in kerosene costs and eliminating 375,000 tons of carbon emissions annually.

Another business inspired by a customer problem is Roger Marsh's Bolt-A-Blok System. Marsh, an engineer with several patents to his credit, was familiar with concrete construction due to his many years as executive director of Indiana's State Highway Commission. Because of his background and training, he could see three problems that needed solutions: 1) unnecessary labor costs, 2) the large volumes of water needed for concrete construction, and 3) the length of time it took for mortar to cure. Marsh improved the standard methods by combining steel with pre-cast blocks. His "ready-built system" uses no water, needs no special equipment, and is strong enough to resist earthquakes and hurricanes. Because build times are drastically reduced, the Bolt-A-Blok System benefits existing commercial needs as well as disaster relief operations and NGOs such as Habitat for Humanity. In 2012, another startup, 3B Construction Solutions, purchased Marsh's award-winning patents, and they are now able to license his technology to construction firms around the world.

A third example of customer want and need is Tommy John underwear. Experiencing the frustration of not having an undershirt that stayed tucked in and that fit well, Tommy Patterson designed a long-tailed undershirt. He surveyed the target of stylish, younger men and determined there was sufficient demand to scale his idea. His research indicated that men were willing to pay more for the luxury of improved fit and feel, and he knew then that a successful business model could be launched. Although his undershirts cost $38, his expanded product line is now carried in over 500 stores nationwide after just three years in business.

6. **Dissect the competition for weakness** – Businesses come and go. Restaurants fail every day. A primary reason for existing business failure is that another entrepreneur has identified a weakness in his competition and has figured out a way to do something better, quicker, or cheaper. For example, Blockbuster went out of business because Netflix's founder, Reed Hastings, was charged $40

for a late DVD. He saw a weakness in the Blockbuster business model, perceived the opportunity for mail order DVDs, and built a successful business on this competitor weakness.

A competitive strategy differentiates from existing models or creates a broader market niche that other companies are not serving. The challenge lies in designing a new model that is different or unique from competitors. Differential advantage could be something as simple as price or quality. For example, when Ruth Fertel purchased the Chris Steak House in New Orleans, she was determined to use only the finest ingredients, serving USDA Prime steaks paired with fine wines in an upscale setting. Her formula worked so well that since franchising in 1977, Ruth's Chris Steak House now has over 140 locations, patronized by loyal customers who appreciate her restaurants' gourmet food and ambiance.

Factors to consider when analyzing the competition are market fragmentation or consolidation, opportunities for an advantage through innovation or technology, customer acquisition costs, and the financial resources of competitors. A key to sustaining market advantage is an economically viable business model (i.e., adequate revenue, profit margins, and healthy cash flow).

7. **Apply the very latest technology to an existing business –** The Palm Pilot handheld organizer was the granddaddy of mobile technology. Introduced in 1996, it was an instant success, selling over one million units in less than two years. At about the same time, Apple developed the Newton, a handheld computer that ran on handwriting recognition software. It flopped, but the Palm built on Newton's weaknesses of price and complexity. Palm Pilot identified the characteristics most important to handheld customers: simplicity, small size, reasonable price, attractive design, and connectivity. The product was built on the customer's

desire for new efficiency, and it led to today's smartphones by taking computer technology handheld and portable.

Today, technology is moving so fast that existing services and products can be made obsolete in nanoseconds. Improvements in ways to transact, transport, or record the full spectrum of commerce are happening daily, and these changes create multiple opportunities for savvy entrepreneurs. Smartphones, for example, have revolutionized function and changed old business models such as booking hotels, reading newspapers, monitoring pets, and paying for merchandise. If you have an idea that will save time or money through the application of technology, test it with many likely users. Smartphone apps are just in their infancy, and developers will continue to find ways to organize our daily activities. Healthcare is a likely growth area for some time to come. The smartphone sector already uses tech to report vital signs and transfer data to medical specialists.

Apple is the classic example of a technology ecosystem. Its products are based on breakthrough innovation revolving around tech platforms, and they reinvented themselves by introducing the App Store, which has become the marketplace for third-party applications. Zillow and Amazon have also used platforms as springboards for complementary services (Amazon Prime, flat fee MLS service), new marketplaces (from books to "the everything store"), and additional networks for third-party business (Amazon sells cloud storage space). Technology trends are accelerating and portend new demands for goods and services that cannot be imagined at present. Global positioning satellites alone have spurred demand for new services and products for customers as diverse as backpackers, mobile phone users, and drivers caught in rush hour traffic. One surefire way to apply technology is to engage in international trade using the web-based tools now in place. Amazon, eBay, Alibaba and other domain marketplaces sell around the world. The Internet expands the number of niches and markets providing significant multiplication of product-fit combinations.

By far the best example of technology applied to a new business model is the story of Walmart. Sam Walton knew discount retailing inside and out, having spent several years in variety stores such as JCPenney and Ben Franklin. He struck out on his own at a time when the Woodland UPC barcode was being introduced to inventory control. This simple technology enabled computer scanning and automated tracking of retail goods on a massive scale. This, in turn, allowed Walmart to efficiently and effectively grow exponentially by using this technology to track inventory and restock their shelves.

8. **Copycat a successful entrepreneur and make improvements –** The key to succeeding with a copycat business is to replicate a proven business concept and bring it to a new or underserved market. Innovation can be expensive, and many consultants believe that originality is overrated and much riskier. They argue that it makes more sense to learn from another company's mistakes and then make incremental improvements.

A potential entrepreneur picks a dynamic, successful entrepreneur in an industry with a good future, and he or she works as a protégé (volunteer, intern, part-time worker, team member) to learn on the job, intending to start a similar kind of business in the future. While working inside a chosen industry, the protégé watches, learns, and tries to become an expert in the field. It can be an established, high-profile company or it can be a viable, recent startup. The latter option of a new company with a successful business model gives a potential entrepreneur the opportunity to grow with the company from the ground floor. Simple timing of employment at Microsoft made over 2,000 millionaires as the company expanded to global proportions.

Another benefit of a copycat plan is the money that can be saved while serving as a protégé. Not only do aspirants observe the industry of the mentor, they also become knowledgeable about the service or product niche while getting paid, setting aside salary, and living beneath their means. Some of the savings can later be used as bootstrap funding when time and opportunity present themselves to start their own companies.

9. **Act as a middleman or work what is known as broker-age** – Here, entrepreneurs provide trade as a service on behalf of clients. Think real estate agents, insurance agencies, or manufacturer representative. A middleman is a self-employed person transacting for his or her customers or clients. A manufacturer rep, for example, is known as an independent sales representative who sells a manufacturer's products to wholesale and retail customers. They usually represent more than one manufacturing firm but generally limit themselves to a manageable number. This method has proved cost-effective for the producer versus using their own personnel. In the case of real estate and insurance agencies, the incentive of closing a sale maximizes sales production.

Because the middleman or broker understands the market by attending conferences, educational seminars, and trade shows, he or she can often work more effectively than salaried personnel. Brokers become adept at solving the problems of end customers and provide a vital link in the product distribution channel. The barriers to entry are low. Frequently, a new broker or middleman can negotiate a contract to represent a producer/manufacturer with one or two client accounts from which they build more. With their sole focus on selling, brokers can target new customers that producers have overlooked. If they are good at interpersonal relations and willing to work hard, their chances to succeed are excellent.

10. **Build on proven templates** – Once the idea for a service or a product has been chosen, it is easier and more cost effective to adopt a proven structure for a successful small business than to re-invent the wheel, so to speak. The following choices speed success in a new startup and are based on the experience of what works and what does not.

Selecting the type of legal structure best suited for a business is an early priority. Entrepreneurs can choose to operate as a proprietorship, a partnership, or as a corporation, but the best choice for a startup is a hybrid structure called a limited liability company or LLC. There are two main benefits to an LLC. The first is pass-through taxation. This means that profits are only taxed as personal income instead of the double taxation that corporations must pay (corporate and personal taxes). The second benefit an LLC provides is a vital safeguard against risk. It establishes a "corporate veil" that puts an owner's financial liability behind a corporate shield. This protects the owner's personal assets in the event of business losses or lawsuits. Every insurance policy written contains exclusions, and lawsuits often can be without merit. Therefore, every business owner should have this line of defense. Operating as an LLC also projects a professional image to the buying public and helps others take a startup more seriously. In addition, an LLC designation is easy to obtain, and the fees are the least expensive among the options. LLC status requires much less administrative paperwork and annual reporting than a corporation, thereby allowing a new owner more time to spend expanding his or her business.

A related legal choice involves intellectual property. All entrepreneurs should consider protecting a new venture's proprietary information. The US Patent and Trademark Office (USPTO) in Washington, DC provides three types of protection: trademarks, copyrights, and patents. A trademark typically protects brand names and logos used on goods as well as services (e.g., Coca-Cola, KFC, and LinkedIn). A copyright protects an original artistic or literary work such as song lyrics or works of fiction. A patent protects an invention, a manufacturing process, or a new design for an existing product. Approximately 90 percent of patents issued are called utility patents or "patents for invention," and they can exclude others from infringing for up to 20 years. What is important to know is patents are detailed, take time, and are expensive to obtain (usually needing an agent or attorney to help with the process). Also, do not confuse web domain names with trademarks. Web addresses are registered with an accredited domain name registrar and not the USPTO. For more information, visit http://www.uspto.gov/inventors/assessment.

A third proven template is to systematize finances from the beginning. At first, use bookkeeping software such as Quicken to keep track of expenses, payments, and revenues. As your business grows, add accounting software such as QuickBooks. The combined cost for both of these easy to learn and well-known programs is under $300, and all data is stored *on premises*. However, the trend seems to be moving toward cloud-based programs such as Sage 50 (formerly Peachtree), which likewise offer a full suite of features. Systematizing allows you to quickly gather and review your company sales, track payroll deductions, produce monthly trial balances, and generate professional looking invoices. Business software also greatly expedites your year-end tax preparation because you can download your organized records directly to your accountant in a matter of minutes.

A fourth recommended template is the team concept for staffing. Teams are proven more efficient in accomplishing tasks, and having compatible, diversified members multiplies skill sets. Teams also increase learning opportunities and cross training so others can fill in for absent members.

Synergy, which is the collaboration of two entities to create an outcome greater than the sum, makes any product more dynamic. The process of brainstorming is built into this model. Think of the accomplishments by these combinations: Jobs and Wozniak (Apple) and Brin and Page (Google).

And lastly, a fifth template for long-term success is an owner's ability to maintain a life/work balance regardless of circumstances. Many entrepreneurs burn out long before they have become successful. Others fail to realize the potential of their ideas because their startup ventures become too frenzied and hectic. Reliance on technology, for example, can become a double-edged sword. Although the Internet vastly increases your reach, access to social media like Facebook, Linkedin, and Twitter can blur the boundaries between when you are working and when you are not. Ultimately, the pressure of being in charge of everything takes a toll.

Unfortunately, I learned this lesson the hard way. After four years of intense pressure starting a commercial insurance agency in metro Atlanta during the most competitive premium period in decades—termed a "soft market"—I developed health problems and had to drink a dozen cups of coffee just to get up steam. Responsibility for twelve employees and $7 million in premiums had gotten to me. Had I been smarter, I might have moderated work and balanced my life more. Two years after selling the agency, I reduced my workload, and my health returned to normal. The demands of a startup should be limited by the requisites for healthy living: proper sleep, good nutrition, exercise, and adequate family and leisure time. Most new ventures are 24/7 when launched, but after they get off the ground, discipline is needed to maintain stability. Stress is a signal to start delegating responsibilities. Above all, entrepreneurship requires resilience and stamina.

An important way to achieve this life/work balance is to adopt personal time management practices. I recommend the plan-goals-and-activities system (PGA). The entrepreneur creates annual, quarterly, weekly, and daily goals and tasks to meet objectives with deadlines that lead to success. Frequently, the entrepreneur needs to prioritize these goals and tasks hourly in order to keep the most important ones in motion. This single technique of working on the most important task for that time can double or triple the chance for success. More details on organizational skills and management style will be presented in Chapter Twelve.

11. **Choose a field with repeat sales** – There is nothing better than having some form of product or service that renews. Start a business that has built-in cycles such as repeat sales due to the nature of the product or service. Think consumer disposal products—razor blades, soap, toilet paper—and services that are ongoing. One of the beautiful facets of the commercial property casualty insurance business was its built-in renewal structure. Every client business had to renew its coverage of worker's compensation and auto liability at least once a year. If an agent entrepreneur did a good job and kept his product competitive, he would enjoy a long-term relationship. One client builds on another, and the business successfully grows upon a foundation for the long haul. For instance, a manufacturer's rep might have the toll position on an expensive piece of oil drilling equipment that has to be replaced every year. Intrinsic, repeat sales give a business forward momentum and make finding new clients less important.

In summary, the basic High Percentage Model is a startup service business differentiated from others who do the same thing begun on a shoestring budget that meets a customer need discovered through a deep consumer dive focused on a narrow target segment. Look at the competition in this space and see what is working and popular. Copycat a successful model using proven templates. Do the customer development necessary to discover an unmet need.

My own experience in starting a commercial insurance agency in a city with a hundreds of other agents was successful because it was based on an exclusive, less expensive product intentionally sold to only three target businesses. The bootstrap was my wife's salary, and the Jacksonville insurance market clearly had room for a new way of marketing commercial insurance (direct writer policies with high-value service). Warren Buffet started his company by investing for family and friends, Richard Branson by selling records by mail, and Elon Musk by marketing an Internet city guide. Look where they started, and you can see how a good idea with a receptive market can launch entrepreneurship.

High Percentage Model Components:

1. Choose a service vs. product business.
2. Use a type of bootstrapping.
3. Refine a service or create a new target.
4. Solve an existing customer complaint.
5. Iterate target to find an unmet need.
6. Dissect competition for weakness.
7. Apply technology to an existing business.
8. Copycat, improve a successful entrepreneur.
9. Act as a middleman or brokerage.
10. Build on proven templates.
11. Choose a field with repeat sales.

Takeaway from Chapter Six

Lessen your startup risk by listening carefully to customers and learning from the experience of others.

CHAPTER SEVEN

Use the Combo Plan

Failing to plan is planning to fail.

— *Alan Lakein*
Author of How to Get Control of Your Time and Your Life

Every business needs a plan. Whether it's a pure startup, a franchise, or a brokerage, whether web-based, licensed, or acquired, there has to be a framework before a new venture is launched. For many years the traditional business plan was the gold standard. A value proposition was described, management, marketing, and competition were analyzed, and the financial capital was forecast into the future. Business schools taught heavy planning, industry research, and lots of procedures. Traditional business plans, however, are built on assumptions about future developments. Boxer Mike Tyson infamously said about his opponents' prefight strategies, "Everybody has a plan until they get punched in the mouth." In other words, unpredictability takes over when the startup begins. It took the technology revolution to pound some sense into the heads of conventional entrepreneurship educators. Credit for this belongs to several people, among them Lean Startup guru Steve Blank, who launched his own series of tech companies in Silicon Valley, made a lot of money, and then reflected on the process he had just experienced. He discovered there were some common characteristics among his eight startups, and most of them germinated from changes made after critical customer feedback. One of Blank's students, Eric Ries, integrated his work into the Lean Startup movement, which is rapidly becoming the favored method to use for a new venture startup.

A business can launch off the minimum viable product (MVP) that customers find attractive and continue as a process until customers suggest enough corrective action to find the one product that clicks. Blank calls this process "customer validation." It allows beginning entrepreneurs to minimize their risk and find an idea that has a much greater chance of sustaining success before it scales or before large amounts of capital are invested. The motto for this startup method is "Fail fast and fail often." The more rapidly a potential idea is redirected by feedback or stopped for lack of interest, the faster the entrepreneur can find an idea with a better chance of working.

One shouldn't perceive the Lean Startup method and the traditional business plan as being mutually exclusive. In reality, a new business benefits from using both systems. Each has its place in new venture development: the learn startup is needed at the beginning, and the traditional business plan is effective during the second stage of the startup cycle. There is good reason for using both, and we encourage readers to integrate them into a single system.

Startup entrepreneurship is all about money. After all, the primary reason to be in business is to make profit. At some point, which we hope is sooner rather than later, the new venture must reach that magnificent place, the breakeven point, where revenues begin to cover the expenses and profits begin to flow. Because it takes time to build clientele, establish a brand, and acquire customers, investors recognize there is a reasonable period of time with no profit. A rule of thumb is a business should become profitable by the end of the second year or some kind of change is necessary. Consequently, both planning systems have to emphasize finances, including the raising of capital, accounting for expenditures, and forecasting future revenue and expenses.

What to seek when planning a new venture is either a differentiated business model or a new business model altogether. There simply is no other way for a new entrepreneur to enter the flow of commerce running through the economy without something that shakes up the existing way of doing business. Think of this commerce of goods and services as flowing through the economy in one gigantic pipeline; your goal is to divert a small portion of this flow through your own smaller pipe. You do that either by changing the way a product is made, marketed, or serviced or by inventing an entirely new product or service. An example of changing an existing product or service would be Uber, the ridesharing service started in San Francisco in 2009. At first they offered only full-sized luxury cars for hire, but their UberX program made smaller vehicles available to customers in 2012. The old model of taxicabs was displaced by Uber's model of using privately-owned vehicles and drivers. This idea is an example of a business model innovation.

An entirely new business model is inventing something that people did not know they needed, has never existed before, and does not have an existing model to follow. One such example is the smartphone. When IBM and Blackberry developed the first Internet-capable phone, there were only basic phones that allowed talk and text and little else. The concept of a computerized phone with applications like iTunes that functioned inside a smartphone and was synchronized with other devices was truly revolutionary. Steve Jobs and his Apple team wrote software, designed functions, and created a new business model in communication. A *Popular Mechanics* survey rated the invention of the smartphone as the most powerful innovations of all time.[17] If you question that statement, consider that hundreds of millions of people around the world no longer have a need for customary banking services thanks to smartphones.

For many years, the traditional business plan has been the primary tool for creating new ventures, and it consisted of nine sections:

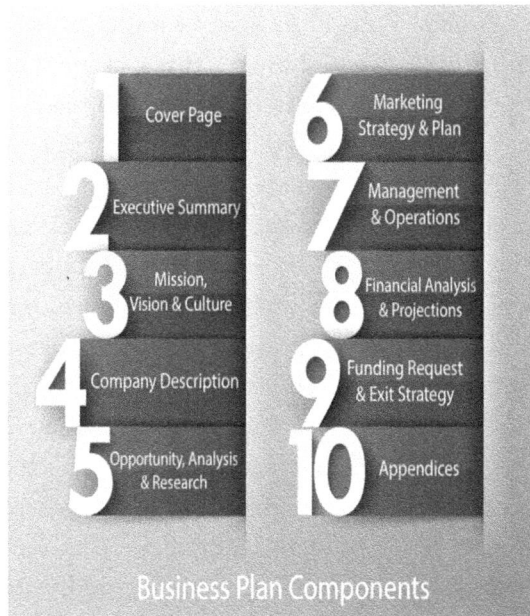

1 Cover Page
2 Executive Summary
3 Mission, Vision & Culture
4 Company Description
5 Opportunity, Analysis & Research
6 Marketing Strategy & Plan
7 Management & Operations
8 Financial Analysis & Projections
9 Funding Request & Exit Strategy
10 Appendices

Business Plan Components

---

[17] Popular Mechanics, "101 Gadgets That Changed the World," 2011, http://www.popularmechanics.com/technology/gadgets/reviews/g165/101-gadgets-that-changed-the-world/?slide=101.

The business plan includes many components—a cover page, executive summary, company description, opportunity analysis and research, marketing strategy, management and operations, financial analysis and projections, a funding request and exit, and an appendix—and takes considerable time to write. Its goal is to add exceptional value to an end user and meet a significant need of the customer. The plan is needed to borrow money and to secure equity financing, and it is used when planning is reliable, assumptions can be made, and analysis is more certain. Preparation of the traditional business plan is time-consuming. It takes months of research, and can easily be based on false assumptions. Aspiring entrepreneurs can spend a year or more writing their plans and chasing investors only to launch their businesses and find out their ideas are invalid and do not meet a market need. This is why a formal business plan can be more useful at a later stage of company growth.

The Lean Startup method offers planners an alternative, quick-response, risk-assessment tool when a comparative business model does not exist, the idea or concept is new, and there is no proven market. It uses evidence and customer feedback to adjust direction when the value of an idea is unknown. Babson College, a leader in academic entrepreneurship, calls the process "CreAction . . . A reasoning that blends creating and action—to propel the entrepreneurial thinker forward."[18]

CreAction is based on the resources at hand, using only what one can afford to lose. By listening to potential customers and searching for a business model, the entrepreneur evaluates, adjusts, reevaluates, and keeps failing until a successful approach is found. Action leads to market reaction, which then refines an idea for a new product or a better service. As problems come up, their solutions will reveal an idea's competitive advantage over rivals. In other words, by talking to prospective customers over and over, a patient entrepreneur will eventually be rewarded.

By using the lean methodology, new startups can avoid the high cost of getting a first customer and the high cost of getting a product wrong. Lean methodology produces products for customers more quickly and cheaply than traditional business planning and, most importantly, minimizes the

---

[18] Charles F. Kiefer, Leonard A. Schlesinger, and Paul B. Brown, *Action Trumps Everything: Creating What You Want in an Uncertain World*, (Duxbury, MA: Black Ink Press, 2010).

risks taken by an entrepreneur. Less upfront cost, more certainty about demand, and refinement of what the market really wants all lower the risk of failure and financial loss. For these reasons I recommend use of the Lean Startup for all new ventures, both proven business models—my insurance agency businesses duplicated long before me—and/or unknown business models—the Uber private rideshare that reinvented a new way of doing an old business.

Another contributor to the Lean Startup revolution is Ash Maurya, a web-based product designer who tweaked the business model canvas (BMC) to the Lean Startup, renaming it the Lean Canvas (see illustration below).

Problem	Solution	Unique Value Proposition	Unfair Advantage	Customer Segments
Top 3 problems	Top 3 features **3**	Single, clear, compelling message that states why you are different and worth buying	Can't be easily copied or bought **7**	Target customers
1	Key Metrics — Key activities you measure **6**	**2**	Channels — Path to customers **4**	**1**
Cost Structure — Customer Acquisition Costs, Distribution Costs, Hosting, People, etc. **5**		Revenue Streams — Revenue Model, Life Time Value, Revenue, Gross Margin **5**		

Lean Canvas is adapted from The Business Model Canvas (http://www.businessmodelgeneration.com) and is licensed under the Creative Commons Attribution-Share Alike 3.0 Un-ported License.

He gave the nine BMC building blocks new names to adapt the canvas to the Lean Startup model: problem, solution, key metrics, value proposition, unfair advantage, channels, customer segments, cost structure, and revenue streams. "Key partners, activities, and resources" were changed in the BMC to "problem, solution, and key metrics to measure," and "customer relationships" became "unfair advantage," aspects of the business not easily copied or bought. It was only natural for Maurya to be the person to make these changes because of his work in web and Internet design. Technology startups need prototype testing to establish value. It is all about generating an idea for a disruptive product or service. It does so by exploring scientific breakthroughs or global trends and then innovating digital improvements to everyday activities. First, a hypothesis is beta tested (traffic is driven to a website). From this data, feedback from early adopters within the target market is gathered, and bugs and glitches are corrected. Next, a minimum viable product (MVP) is produced. In keeping with the lean method, this process is done with little risk or money until the idea's worth is demonstrated. With a minimum viable product, a tech entrepreneur can then launch a product and continue to engage the potential customer and pivot or iterate as needed.

A good example of a traditional business plan was the one created by American industrialist Henry Ford. While he did not invent the automobile, he developed and manufactured the first affordable car. Along the way he evolved from being an apprentice machinist in Detroit to a builder and designer, creating the Quadricycle and 88-horsepower 999 raced by Barney Oldfield. He then shifted to the mass production of the breakthrough Model T. Always innovating, speeding up manufacturing, and lowering prices, Ford also brought us the first modern franchise system of dealerships, the five-dollar workday, and an employee profit sharing plan. The five-dollar workday nearly doubled what workers were making at the time. It proved profitable by reducing turnover, raising production, and enabling workers to afford the cars they were producing.

The aforementioned Sara Blakely is an example of a person who used the Lean Startup. She was selling fax machines door-to-door and had to wear pantyhose in the hot Florida climate. Disliking the look of a seam on her open-toed shoes but liking the body control of the top, she cut off the feet of her pantyhose and achieved her desired result. The pantyhose continuously rolled up her legs, however, so she created a product that did not have seamed toes. Blakely researched hosiery, developed a prototype, and over the period of a year used her mother and friends to test ideas. Among other "iterations" to industry standard she made were different waistbands for different sized customers, packaging in red vs. the standard beige color, and using the name Spanx based on sound and ease of trademark registration. At a meeting with a sales rep for Neiman Marcus stores, Blakely changed into her product in the ladies restroom in the presence of the buyer to demonstrate its benefits. The redesigned pantyhose represented her minimum viable product, and the Neiman Marcus order was just the beginning of department store sales (Bloomingdales and Saks soon followed). At the scalability stage of growth, Blakely hired a ten-year Coca-Cola veteran as CEO who focused on higher quality, brand recognition, and fast growth. Along the way, marketing was helped by Blakely's appearance on the *Oprah Winfrey Show.* At the time, she was still a fax machine salesperson. *Forbes* labeled Blakely the youngest self-made female billionaire.

New entrepreneurs should rely on the Lean Startup approach until they reach the point where their idea has found a minimum viable product that can be sustained in the market. When it is apparent there is a solid, ongoing market for the product or service, it is time to standardize operating procedures. In the second stage of the startup lifecycle, a traditional business plan should be completed. Investors will not lend money without an organized presentation about the venture. The business plan gives them about ten to fifteen pages using the sections shown on page 55.

A Startup Financing Cycle chart shows two stages of early development after reaching a breakeven point (see illustration).

Startup Financing Cycle

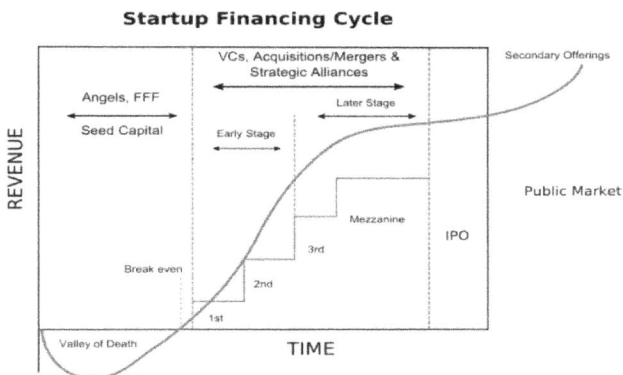

Somewhere in the 1st or 2nd ladder of the Early Stage the hypothesis has been proven, and the product can be scaled (i. e., growth will be sustained). At that point a traditional business plan is needed.

Mary Han's (Ryerson University, Toronto) Entrepreneurial S-Curve (used with permission).

The business plan becomes just as important as the Lean Startup model once the idea has traction (i.e., it is viable, scalable, and sustainable).

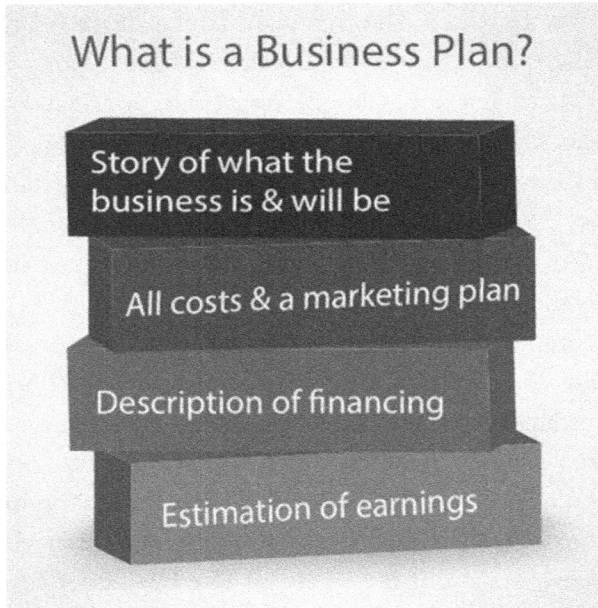

What is a Business Plan?

Story of what the business is & will be

All costs & a marketing plan

Description of financing

Estimation of earnings

Takeaway from Chapter Seven

Use the Lean Startup then switch to the business plan at scale.

CHAPTER EIGHT

Where There Is No Risk, There Is No Reward

The person who risks nothing, does nothing, has nothing, is nothing, and becomes nothing.

— Leo F. Buscaglia
Bestselling Author and Motivational Speaker

We live on a fragile planet with a very hot core, and risk is all around us. Toxins are in our air and water and even in the materials we use to build our houses. Accidents can occur at all times and in the most unlikely places. In short, if you are alive today on planet Earth, you cannot escape risk. All you can do is take precautions, reduce exposure to risk, and, as the Brits were advised during World War II, "Keep Calm and Carry On."

No doubt entrepreneurship can be scary because it almost always involves some financial commitment. There are ways to diminish potential risk, however, and increase the probability for success. A major benefit of the new lean method is that it keeps money or resource needs minimal until the idea has been validated. By using resources at hand only in an amount one can afford to lose, the idea can be shaped by customer feedback until a scalable product is found and more resources can be safely committed. Risk by itself can actually have a positive effect. It can add an element of excitement and a sense of richness to any undertaking. Choosing the road less traveled will engage more of your creativity, logic, and perseverance, and the outcomes thereby will be more deeply satisfying.

Unless you overcome your fear of rejection, you might never meet the person of your dreams. Likewise, you can't get that desired career without taking the risk of being turned down for a first job. Consider that really successful entrepreneurs put it all on the line. They embrace risk-taking. Many of them even started early in life overcoming a fear of failure. A popular proverb goes, "If you do what you've always done, you'll get what you've always gotten." Also, a measure of self-confidence certainly increases the chances for successful entrepreneurship.[19] Thus, the message is clear: an entrepreneur *must* be willing to fail and accept the risk of losing money.

Ted Turner, the "mouth of the South," exemplifies the classic risk-taker. He took over his family's billboard business at age twenty-four after his father committed suicide. By sheer force of will, self-confidence, and innovative thinking, he created an entertainment empire. From a 1963 value of roughly $1 million, Turner Broadcasting System had generated a net worth in excess of $5 billion by the time Turner merged TBS with AOL Time Warner in 1996.

His first move was to purchase an Atlanta UHF station in 1970 and bring the superstation concept to cable television. Before anyone else, Turner came up with the idea of uplinking the broadcast signal to a satellite and sending it back to various cable systems.[20]

He then purchased the Atlanta Braves for broadcast content and turned them into a popular national franchise by putting their games on the Super-station. He launched championship wrestling and invented the Goodwill Games for the same reason. But his biggest coup was in 1980 when Turner created CNN, a 24-hour cable news channel. CNN is currently seen in approximately 100 million cable and satellite households. Round the clock coverage of the Space Shuttle Challenger disaster in 1986 and the first Gulf War in 1991 helped leapfrog CNN past the big three broadcast networks. Still in search of more content for his growing number of cable stations, Turner purchased the MGM/UA film studio in 1986 and then tried unsuccessfully to acquire CBS. Turner Network Television, Turner Classic Movies, and

[19] Maxwell Maltz, *Psycho-Cybernetics: A New Way to Get More Living Out of Life*, (New York: Pocket Books, 1989), 16.
[20] Porter Bibb, *Ted Turner: It Ain't as Easy as It Looks*, (Boulder, CO: Johnson Books, 1997).

the Cartoon Channel followed. His incredibly successful run of business creation slowed when he merged TBS with Time Warner, whose stock promptly collapsed with Turner as the single, largest stockholder. The reason was that dial-up obsolescence caused by the arrival of broadband Internet made AOL's demand drop, illustrating how quickly a business model can fade. As Turner explained, "I went along with the AOL merger with Time Warner, and it was a catastrophe. Supporting the merger was the biggest mistake I made. I did a lot on instinct. It helps to have a little bit of luck too. But mainly, it's a matter of judgment."[21]

Ronald Heifetz of Harvard University's John F. Kennedy School of Government likes to say if you make just one real decision in your life, that's more than most people. That's because making decisions and taking risks requires complete freedom from loyalties, expectations, and fears that fog our risk-versus-reward equations. For example, even though people were cutting household expenses during the Great Depression, refrigerator sales went up 30 percent. Refrigerator sales grew because it was a highly innovative product produced by an industry not afraid to hire people, invest in product, and market itself when others were not.

J. Paul Getty, an oil producer who at one time was the richest man in the world, said he never made a decision without risking everything he had in the process: "There are one hundred men seeking security to one able man who is willing to risk his fortune." Robert Lenzner, who wrote Getty's biography, *The Great Getty*, described his subject as a fascinating and contradictory character. Getty was born in 1892 in Minneapolis, lived a long time in Southern California, and died an expatriate in London. In 1903, his father George traveled across the old Oklahoma Territory trying to collect a debt when he discovered the black gold, oil. His father's drive for success contributed to Getty becoming a loner who spent hours reading the novels of G. A. Henty, an English adventure author whose model for success, which was "to work, to save, and to learn," inspired the young Getty. George invited J. Paul into his Minnehoma Oil Co. after his son struck oil at the Nancy Taylor farm. It has been said that the World War I

---

[21] Aly Weisman, "Ted Turner Reveals His Biggest Business Regret with CNN," *Business Insider,* 2012, http://www.businessinsider.com/ted-turner-wishes-cnn-had-less-fluff-2012-10.

allies floated to victory on a sea of oil, and the fields of Oklahoma enriched the George F. Getty Co. father-son partnership that later became Getty Oil. Getty junior became one of the few independent oilmen to use the relatively young science of geology, and his foresight paid off big.[22]

After making a million dollars (1900 values), Getty returned to California and retired at the ripe age of twenty-five. When his father died in 1930, Getty was elected president of Getty Oil, but final authority rested with his mother and other investors. He used his operational control to acquire companies at a fraction of their cost after the stock market crash. "My stock purchases were financed by every dollar I possessed and every cent of credit I could obtain." One of these takeovers was the Tidewater Oil Company, the ninth largest in the US. "Buy when everyone else is selling, and hold on until everyone else is buying" was the motto Getty used to acquire Tide-water Oil shares virtually unnoticed on the stock exchange in 1932. Thus, he became one of the first modern corporate takeover strategists to use the stock market to gain control of other companies.[23]

In 1949, Getty continued to gamble and take risks and obtained a sixty-year concession in Saudi Arabia's part of the neutral zone, paying $9.5 million in cash for the concession. In 1953, his Saudi interests hit big with oil in excess of 16 million barrels a year, and Getty was elevated into the billionaire class. Before his death, he authored the book *How to Be Rich*, which included several notable quotes: "To build wealth today, you must be in your own business" and "No one can possibly achieve any real and lasting success or get rich in business by being a conformist."[24]

A successful entrepreneur likewise understands that failure is built into the job. Jonathan Mildenhall, chief marketing officer at Airbnb and former head of global marketing for Coca-Cola says, "If you don't have room to fail, you don't have room to grow." The smart or Lean Startup says to fail fast and fail often because ideas should be either refined or eliminated until a scalable product is created. As discussed in Chapter Six, the challenge for an aspiring entrepreneur is to reduce risks associated

---

[22] Lenzner, Robert. *The Great Getty: The Life and Loves of J. Paul Getty.* (New York: Crown Publishers, 1986), 13, 21.
[23] Ibid., 69-76.
[24] Getty, J. P., *How to Be Rich,* (New York: Jove Books, 1983).

with a new venture, and the Lean Startup method provides the roadmap. The process has to be nimble and quick and rely on "agile development."

Only by taking a chance can you overcome the fear of failure, and chances are very good you will learn many lessons and improve your life along the way. Benjamin Disraeli said, "Life is too short to be little." Indeed, it is, and everyone has some gift that can reach its full potential through expression as a new business. No one will ever see that gift nor will you experience the real you without sticking your neck out, taking a calculated risk, and be willing to fail.

Takeaway from Chapter Eight

The biggest risk is not taking one at all.

CHAPTER NINE

Work Hard and Work Smart

There is no such thing as something for nothing.
— *Napoleon Hill*
Author of Think and Grow Rich

Thomas Edison is known for his many inventions, but he is also known for his hard work ethic and perseverance. It was Edison who said good fortune often happens when opportunity meets with preparation. Being your own boss takes effort and determination. Edison set up his first laboratory in 1870 in Newark, and as an independent entrepreneur, he developed products for the highest bidder. One of his biggest customers was Western Union for whom he had worked as a young man. They encouraged him to develop a communication device to compete with Alexander Graham Bell's telephone. What resulted was a method for recording sound known as the phonograph. By far his most famous achievement was a practical electric light bulb. Contrary to popular belief, Edison didn't invent the light bulb. He actually improved on a fifty-year-old idea. It took countless experiments and long hours to finally produce a reliable and long-lasting source of light.

Edison not only brought us the incandescent electric light, but he also designed the entire lighting system needed to make the light bulb safe, practical, and economical, e.g., voltage regulators, safety fuses, insulating materials, and light sockets with on-off switches. What is not so well known is Edison's long road of trial and error. Hundreds of possible filament materials were tried, but Edison never gave up. People would be surprised to know how many Edison inventions failed, among them sound in motion pictures, a method to mine iron ore, and the use of cement in construction.

Our country was founded on the Protestant work ethic, which emphasizes hard work, frugality, and diligence. Ben Franklin said the road to success comes through hard work, determination, and sacrifice. Dale Carnegie advised, "Do the hard jobs first. The easy jobs take care of themselves." He also said, "If you want to conquer fear, don't sit home and think about it. Go out and get busy. Most of the important things in the world have been accomplished by people who have kept on trying when there seemed no hope at all."[25] This sentiment is echoed in Stephen Covey's first habit of highly successful people. They are proactive, causing something to happen versus responding to it after it has happened. Hard work teaches us to push through when times are tough and later provides great satisfaction when success comes. The sense of pride in hard work cannot be replaced with anything else.

My own beginning was one of innocent enthusiasm, committing to as many insurance programs and quotes as possible in the hopes some would result in orders for business. One of my early bosses preached, "Activity breeds activity," and I lived that advice. I simultaneously prospected, serviced, quoted, negotiated, and underwrote. Sending out the aforementioned cause, there is no question an effect returned. At one point I was so overwhelmed with things to do, I shut down my one-man office, drove to the Southside branch of the Jacksonville library, and took about a dozen books off the shelf on the subject of time management. Some of the ideas I wrote down and took back to my office have stuck with me my whole career (and are detailed among the tools in Chapter Ten). The point is hard work must be smart work. Honest, *intelligent* work is almost always rewarded. Working hard is not enough; successful entrepreneurs work on the right activities at the right time.

One practice I developed for smarter work was target marketing three to four specialties simultaneously. By concentrating on just a few types of industrial trades, I was able to learn all I could about innate operations and special exposures. I became familiar with the coverage required, their vulnerable activities, the best insurance markets, and what to look for when reviewing programs. We could then participate in their local association,

---

[25] Dale Carnegie, *How to Stop Worrying and Start Living*, (New York: Pocket Books, 1985).

socialize with owners and managers, and slowly gain a profile among the trade.

Segments chosen for solicitation were service and subcontractors (electricians, plumbers), transportation entities (auto dealers, truckers), rural utilities (electric co-ops, telephone companies), and multi-family dwellings (apartments houses, condominiums). I always had three specialties underway at any one time with a fourth held in abeyance. This diversification protected against a change beyond my control. It ended up actually saving one of my agencies from going out of business.

I specialized in rural electric co-ops from my earlier training working for a large broker. Using an agricultural insurance company based in Colorado, I was able to take advantage of the withdrawal of a national rural electric insurance program from Georgia. I wrote many accounts over several years. I had just closed the two largest accounts when the insurance company decided to drop electrocution as an insurable risk. I was given thirty-five days to notify customers and find an alternate market, virtually impossible because the exposure was so dangerous.

As a consequence, I lost about 40 percent of my written premium, which meant an equal 40 percent of commission income. The only reason I was able to avoid missing a step financially and continue my business without losing staff was because I had started a fourth specialty a year before. We had acquired a large national truck line based in South Atlanta six months earlier by using a rating technique I learned from a mentor called "retrospective rating."

This kind of calculation was done looking back at a particular measure of exposure which, in this case, was payroll. Just as I lost fourteen rural electric co-ops from my book of business, the first six-month premium came due at the trucking account. It turned out to be the largest premium I ever wrote, and its accompanying commission literally saved my agency. Specialization and diversification are always important keys to any successful entrepreneurial startup.

Any legitimate book about entrepreneurship will detail the price an entrepreneur must pay upfront to be successful. There is no escaping a sacrifice at the beginning of a new business venture. It takes unbelievable commitment to get a startup business off the ground. Be prepared to work seven days a week for the first year or two. Only after the business is scaled, viable, and well underway can an entrepreneur ease off the gas pedal. Consider the rewards for working harder than other people for a period of time. Once the cost of doing business has been covered, any amount of revenue above that level is ownership income (i.e., pre-tax income for the owners). At the point your enterprise is self-sustaining and profitable, you can then set your own salary. And if this forward momentum keeps rolling, an entrepreneur can ultimately reap extraordinary wealth.

Among the richest men in the world who benefited from scalable businesses are Carlos Slim of Mexico, whose "surplus" income now amounts to a net worth of $76 billion, and Bill Gates of Microsoft who has accumulated $79 billion. Add to this Warren Buffet of Berkshire Hathaway at $73 billion, Amancio Ortega of Spain at $66 billion, and all four of Sam Walton's children at $38 billion each. These great fortunes were made in demand products, respectively cellular phones, computer software, intrinsic investing, fashion clothing, and discount retail. All are satisfying a broad need by consumers who buy products repeatedly. For example, most of Warren Buffet's companies are consumer nondurables like Coca-Cola and Dairy Queen. So, another secret to successful entrepreneurship is specializing in a repetitively bought product or service. The property casualty insurance business provides a good example of repeat purchase. Businesses are required to carry workers compensation and automobile liability insurance which gave my business model strength versus life insurance, a one-time sale.

The most memorable story about paying a price and impacting the world is that of Wilbur and Orville Wright, the inventors of the airplane. Owners of a Dayton, Ohio, bicycle shop, the brothers gained their mechanical skills by working for years on all manner of machinery. They began to manufacture their own bicycles and used the revenue to fund their interest in flight. There were seven years of continual work, testing, and disappointments before they developed their flying machine into the first practical fixed-wing airplane. From 1900 until the first powered flights in 1903, they conducted glider tests and developed skills as pilots. What seemed to separate the Wright brothers from other experimenters of the time was their use of a homemade wind tunnel that allowed them to collect accurate data and refine their propellers and wings more efficiently.[26]

Like so many entrepreneurs, the brothers' breakthrough came from solving a problem, the *flying problem*. While others focused on more powerful engines, the Wright brothers focused on solving the problem of pilot controls. They were the first to invent aircraft controls that made fixed-wing, powered flight possible. Following the first successful flight, they worked another four years developing a practical airplane. Wilbur noticed in observing birds that they changed the angle of their wing tips to make their bodies turn right or left. To achieve the same effect with man-made wings, he discovered wing warping by twisting a long inner-tube box in the bicycle shop. Sure enough, on their biplane kite, one end produced more lift when the wings were twisted. The invention of three-axis control allowed the pilot to steer and maintain equilibrium, and this became the standard on fixed-wing aircraft. The entire trial and error process was expensive, and since they were neither wealthy nor funded by the government, the decision to withdraw from the bicycle business and focus full time on a practical airplane was a courageous one.

The reward for intelligent work is effective design and utility function, but success also requires the work to be timely as well. Business can be cruel with its inherent bias towards getting the job done, and customers reward those products and services that deliver on their schedules. About the only thing that separated my insurance agency from another was service. We worked eleven-hour days, including weekends, to provide a level superior to the competition. That meant our proposals were competitive, detailed, and usually improved in coverage. A proposal for a medium-sized plumbing company, as an example, might take forty to fifty hours of prep-aration. Pre-qualification of companies to quote became a big consideration because of this time investment. As an agency, we had to be sure the quote would be seriously considered and that we would be treated honestly and fairly. There were no fees for a fifty-hour preparation quote, and if we did not close a reasonable percentage of attempts, results would not be sufficient to stay in business. After all, it does come down to cash flow in a

---

[26] Fred Howard, *Wilbur and Orville: A Biography of the Wright Brothers,* (Mineola, N.Y: Dover Publications, 1998), 335-345.

small business. Entrepreneurs have to keep an eye on their outlays of time and their income on an ongoing basis. Fortunately, most small businesses today have the benefit of a software accounting system that can summarize financial pictures with the click of a mouse.

If you choose the path of entrepreneurship, it is almost like a law of physics that you can't have reward without sacrifice. The saying goes, "The road to success is fraught with distractions and paved with the summations of a myriad of small efforts." Once you decide to try your hand at entrepreneurship, you have decided you are willing to pay the price of success, and you are obligated to go forward with the payment. There are no nine-to-five hour jobs in entrepreneurship. It takes a superior effort to start, build up, and run a successful business. When I look at a healthy small business, I know a lot of blood, sweat, and tears have been invested in it. In order to create a competitive advantage, some aspect of your business has to be better. You will have to wear many hats: be accessible, build a good reputation, create a team, become an expert, get to know your customers, sell, manage, and plan. All of these things take time and organization.

Work Hard and Work Smart:

1. Don't Be Afraid to Fail
2. Intelligent Work Is Always Rewarded
3. Specialize in a Few Target Markets
4. Be Prepared for 24/7 at First
5. Try to Provide a Repeatable/Exhaustible Product
6. Solve a Problem (Like the Wright Bros)
7. Out Service the Competition

Takeaway from Chapter Nine

You will have to pay a hefty price at the beginning.

CHAPTER TEN

People Are Key

*One real relationship in the real world is worth more than
10,000 social media links, likes, or followers.*

— Steven Tobak
Managing Partner, Invisor Consulting

Successful small businesses have one thing in common. Their owners know how to build and maintain personal relationships. Without strong relationships it's impossible to be successful. The Californian consultant Michael Denisoff says, "You need to have long-term customers and good vendor relationships that will carry you through challenging times or tight deadlines, as well as relationships with other business owners to share struggles, resources, and best practices that can really give you an edge."[27]

David Schwartz's spends part of his bestselling book, *The Magic of Thinking Big*, discussing relationships for the same reasons. He says a person either supports you willingly or doesn't support you at all. Rather than being pulled up to a higher job, a person is "lifted up," and they are individuals who are likable and personable. Being likable makes you lighter to lift. So, painful though it might be, if you want to be successful and own your own business, you've got to develop some people skills and make yourself "lighter to lift."[28]

Fortunately, there is a seminal book written to improve human relationships, which is so good I include it in my entrepreneurship course. First

---

[27] Darren Dahl, "How to Build Better Business Relationships," *Inc.*, 2011,
http://www.inc.com/guides/201101/how-to-build-better-business-relationships.html.
[28] David J. Schwartz, *The Magic of Thinking Big*, (New York: Simon & Schuster, 1987).

published in 1937, *How to Win Friends and Influence People* by Dale Carnegie has sold over 20 million copies, because its basic understanding of human nature will never be outdated. The book is a people skills bible. Carnegie wrote that financial success is built from 15 percent professional knowledge and 85 percent an "ability to express ideas, to assume leadership, and to arouse enthusiasm among people."[29] The book's guidelines that apply to entrepreneurship are: arouse in others an eager want, people crave appreciation and recognition, actively research the other person's interests, agree with the other person's point of view, give honest and sincere appreciation, talk in terms of the other person's interest, smile, become genuinely interested in other people, and remember the other person's name is to them the sweetest and most important sound in any language.

Consider how many daily business activities depend on personal relationships: team building, marketing success, company morale, customer relations, and public relations. Two critical relationships for an entrepreneur are those of mentor and spouse. Countless startups have relied on the advice of a good mentor and the support of a loyal spouse. Endearing these special relationship is essential to the success of many new ventures. Getting employees or associates to willingly do what you want is another vital skill dependent almost entirely on goodwill and personal relationships. Respect for their work, concern for their family, and encouragement at the right time contributes directly to your bottom line by making employees happy.

A master entrepreneur who founded over a dozen companies and made millions of dollars is Jack Nadel. I first saw Nadel on the Fox Business Channel promoting his book, *The Evolution of an Entrepreneur*. His title alone piqued my interest, so I ordered the book and fell in love with its practicality and simple message. Nadel's entrepreneurial journey started after the end of World War II. As a bombardier in the US Army Air Corps, he saw the opportunity for importing and exporting goods between the United States and Asia. After returning to Los Angeles, his first deal was dyeing army drab material navy blue to sell to the Chinese. Today, his company, Jack Nadel International, has twenty-five offices around the

---

[29] Dale Carnegie, *How to Win Friends and Influence People*, (New York: Pocket Books, 1998).

world, employs hundreds of people, and is a leader in the field of brand advertisement and marketing.

What I particularly like about Nadel's book are his fifty best tips for surviving and thriving in business. They are based on his school of hard knocks, and each one is explained with details and specific examples. He includes advice about business relationships among his best tips. My favorites are: "All business is personal"; "The three Rs of business success are Relationships, Results, and Rewards"; "Silence is golden. Listen, learn, and prosper"; "Don't let your ego get in the way"; "Find ways to agree as early as you can in a negotiation"; "Taking a partner is like getting married"; and "Honesty is not only the best policy, it's the most profitable one."[30] After starting many companies and looking back over a long career, Nadel knows that relationships, listening to others, less ego, points for agreement, and honesty are essential to success. On a trade mission to Japan for President Reagan, he was struck by a comment from Akio Morita, the President of Sony: "The problem we have with America is that you come over here and want to make a deal. We meet you and want to form a relationship from which we can make many deals."[31]

Another important part of human relations within the realm of entrepreneurship is to have some fun. If you are passionate about your idea, product, or service, doing it every day can bring a lot of pleasure. Looking back on my three businesses, the enjoyment was the journey. Overcoming obstacles, meeting interesting and colorful people, and forging close relationships all enriched my life. In addition, any advancements or monetary gains I was able to provide others along the way were personally gratifying. When it comes to entrepreneurship and fun, it would be difficult to find a better role model than Richard Branson. A native of Surrey, England, Sir Richard launched Virgin Records in 1973. Today, the Virgin Group operates more than two hundred companies in over thirty countries. In his words, "You don't learn to walk by following rules. You learn by doing, and by falling over."

---

[30] Jack Nadel, *The Evolution of an Entrepreneur*, (Santa Monica, CA: JNJ Publishing, LLC, 2013).
[31] Ibid.

What makes his success all the more remarkable is he is dyslexic and dropped out of school at sixteen to start a magazine. To help fund the magazine, Branson started a mail-order record company called Virgin. Next came his first record shop in London where he began producing records on the Virgin label from his own studio. Bitten by the entrepreneurial bug, Branson expanded his work to a travel company, a transatlantic airline, and a chain of Virgin megastores. Like most entrepreneurs, he hit a financial bump in the road and was forced to pull back, selling Virgin records for a billion dollars (some say to finance the airline). His timing proved propitious with the arrival of digitally-streamed music. Since then he has added a railroad company, a game preserve, a mobile phone company, domestic airlines in the US and Australia, and, recently, a space tourism company. Ever the adventurer, Branson has announced that he and his son and daughter would be passengers on Virgin Galactic's first public flight to outer space.

Good people skills are also vital for successful negotiations. It is inevitable that startups have to bargain with all manner of suppliers, personnel, service providers, and sellers in the process of building a business. The more likable and open-minded you are, the better it will go. Most people go into negotiations hell bent on looking after their own interests, only to find that the other party is doing exactly the same thing. The result is mutual escalation of conflict. Try to see negotiation as getting your interests met through an agreement versus an alternative. Positions are what we want, and interests are why we want them so we try to negotiate the *why* and not the *what*. Understand the interests of the other side so you can focus on mutual benefits. One of Stephen Covey's "seven habits" advises to think "win-win" and to seek first to understand the other party and then to be understood.[32] Active listening is a big part of successful negotiations, and Dale Carnegie's respect for the other person's point-of-view goes a long way. Frame the discussion positively as a joint endeavor. Find issues of low value you can trade which are high value to the other side.

If negotiations fail and an agreement cannot be reached, negotiators turn to what is known professionally as the "Best Alternative to a Negotiated

---

[32] Stephen R. Covey, *The 7 Habits of Highly Effective People*, (New York: Free Press, 2004).

Agreement" or BATNA, a concept developed by Roger Fisher and William Ury, two Harvard researchers. The BATNA approach seeks a non-adversarial way to resolve an impasse. You start by making informed assumptions about the other side's BATNA and doing your best to evaluate its weaknesses. Next, develop a list of options you might consider if no agreement is reached. A strong BATNA position with viable alternatives gives you the power to walk away. Focus on asking questions about mutual interests and propose flexible, attainable alternatives. Finally, always promote the benefits to be realized by accepting your offer.[33]

Takeaway from Chapter Ten

All business is personal
so make yourself easy to lift.

---

[33] Roger Fisher, William Ury, and Bruce Patton, *Getting to Yes: Negotiating Agreement without Giving In*, (New York: Penguin, 2011).

CHAPTER ELEVEN

Selling Is a Value Proposition

The aim of Marketing is to know and understand the Customer so well that the product or service fits him and sells itself.
— *Peter Drucker*

Many first time entrepreneurs make the mistake of investing in superfluous objectives to launch a business, but customers are indispensable to a nascent business. New business owner's efforts should be focused on designing their product or service with the right buyers in mind. The focus on customer needs is the essence of the Lean Startup method. The importance of customers is why planning a marketing strategy should be an early priority. At the most basic level, a business owner uses marketing to invest time, resources, and money to say good things about her business. Public relations—press releases, community service, independent reviews—is when the entrepreneur lets others do it for her. PR is sometimes called "earned media." A successful company needs both kinds of promotion. Likewise, you need to use both traditional media such as newspapers, radio, and direct mail as well as Internet outlets such as a company website, online publications, and social media: Facebook, Craigslist, and YouTube. Whatever mix you choose, be sure to put most of your marketing dollars toward reaching current customers. Frequently, businesses spend too much money advertising to attract new customers. Instead, it's better to strengthen relationships with the customers you already have because their trust will result in the best kind of advertising there is: word of mouth. It's very persuasive, it travels fast, and it's free!

As with so many other aspects of entrepreneurship, "focus" is the operative word for successful marketing. How does your business add value? Does it offer superior service, reliability, product quality, expertise, or convenience? Your promotional efforts need to convey this added value. For example, our rural telephone insurance business was marketed through memberships in the telephone associations of five Southeastern states. We attended their annual conventions, networked all members, and promoted our agency as an official vendor specializing in their industry. We used personal selling as our method of marketing, and this one-on-one prospecting allowed us to explain our expertise to an already select audience. There are many benefits of a specialty field for a small business. It is one of the reasons why a newcomer should choose a niche product to market to a narrow target. It significantly improves the chances for success.

Reaching targeted customers online is another matter entirely. These days, competition for "clicks" and "eyeballs" is intense and ever-expanding. Creativity and new skills are required, because it is all too easy for your online presence to be either lost in the crowd or ineffective. Start with good website design. It should be user-centric and appeal to the needs of the user. Steve Krug, a well-known information architect and user-experience professional, has a basic rule for web design: "Don't make me think."[34] Since users tend to scan text rapidly, information should be brief, easy to digest, and artfully arranged. Good web design also adheres to the "three click rule," which means users will be able to find the information they seek within three clicks.

Another necessary feature is search engine optimization (SEO) because it provides ongoing free and targeted advertising. When people search for what your business offers, SEO will *organically* rank your website at the top of the results page. Unless you are familiar with such terms as meta tags, algorithms, and keywords, you will need technical support to set this up, but it will be money well spent. Recent studies indicate a first-page ranking captures 33 percent of search traffic. A second-page ranking attracts only half this number, and "click-throughs" quickly drop off for succeeding

---

[34] Steve Krug, *Don't Make Me Think, Revisited: A Common Sense Approach to Web Usability*, (San Francisco, CA: New Riders, Peachpit, Pearson Education, 2014).

pages. Refer to Dr. Andy Williams's *SEO 2015 & Beyond* for more information about SEO.

Driving a high volume of traffic to your website is a great achievement, but is really only the beginning of a successful marketing campaign. Next you must elicit a strong reaction to your brand's product or service. You need to articulate your commitment to excellence and company values so that an emotional bond will form with the visitor. A brilliant example of this is the marketing campaign used for Nest, a revolutionary thermostat. The product's simplicity of operation, its cool design, and its unique features were the result of careful attention to the smallest product and branding details. Nest perfectly conveyed its company's values, especially the environmental benefits, and the strong buzz led initial inventory to sell out quickly. The growth was almost exclusively word-of-mouth from reviews, requests, and feedback from customers. A second generation Nest thermostat operates from a smartphone application.

Three considerations when marketing a small business startup are selection of a target market, deciding how to segment that market, and creating a unique position within it. Your target must be attractive, and you have to have the ability to meet its demand. By focusing on a specific trade or niche, you can become an expert, as I did in casualty insurance risks. Use your skills and background to mesh with the target, and if necessary acquire an expertise to serve it and talk their language.

Try applying the market segmentation method within the market: geographic (population by location), demographic (gender, income, age, etc.), psychographic (lifestyle differences such as opinion, politics, etc.), and behavioral (observations, price attractiveness, etc.). With limited resources you may choose to target only one or two segments of the whole market and find the growth space inside the market.

You'll want to develop a marketing plan based on your vision and analysis of the customer. This plan is based on research both primary and secondary, and nothing replaces the importance of customer development as used in lean startup and agile development (Chapters Six and Seven). Let the end user determine the specifics for your service or product based on what they tell you they want to have to satisfy their needs.

Think about competitive advantage as you plan. What distinguishes your product or service in the mind of your target market and provides the difference they want to have? It's hard to beat the old fashioned "four P's" of the marketing mix—product, price, place, and promotion—when looking for a competitive advantage. Meet a customer need, price the product low enough to sell but high enough to make a profit, choose a location that reaches the target the best, and promote its popularity by all means that reach the end user. Publicity is free and great.

Choose your target segment carefully because with limited resources you want to be as well aligned with the market as possible. As you test your ideas with a potential customer, it may be necessary to redefine your target according to what the customer tells you will or will not work. Use the nine-section business model canvas to find the right product-market fit and the right sweet spots for profit, resources, selling channels, and key activities. Above all, build a brand through any of these: logo, name, reputation, personality, ethical standards, treating employees well, association with charity, and an active community involvement.

A final note of caution about marketing in general: the global economy has always been a dynamic entity, and in the twenty-first century, the pace of change will continue to accelerate. Your business cannot afford to stand pat while everything else is in motion. Make sure you pay attention to the metrics of your marketing campaigns and find out what your customers are saying about you. Over time, your business's added value may lose its appeal, and quick course corrections will be needed. Remember, a unique business idea requires a sustainable competitive advantage serving a targeted market segment. Talk to your potential customers—get "outside the building"—so you know their needs and wants better than they do themselves.

Takeaway from Chapter Eleven

Stay focused on identifying, reaching, persuading, and satisfying your customers.

CHAPTER TWELVE

Mastering the Tools
and Putting It All Together

The mechanic that would perfect his work must first sharpen his tools.

— Confucius

The best tool, of course, is the Lean Startup. It has become *the* major leap forward in new venture planning, and everyone up to the point of a viable and sustainable business should use it. There are other important rules, however, for self-employment to share here. Some are based on lessons I learned the hard way, and others are best practices for small businesses. Previously, I touched on the day early in my first agency when I left the office overwhelmed and desperately needing to learn something about time management. I knew I needed better organization, but I had no idea how to go about it. From a dozen books at the Jacksonville Public Library, I wrote down twenty-five rules for time management. Among them were the practices of waste basketry (handle a piece of paper only once and toss everything possible), use of a "quiet hour," the batching of similar tasks, setting priorities, and the importance of the Pareto principle (20 percent of your clients will generate 80 percent of your sales).

I also started practicing telephone discipline. Rather than answering my office phone whenever it rang, I began religiously taking calls between 8:45 a.m. and 11 a.m. so that clients and underwriters would always know when they could reach me. After 11 a.m. I asked my secretary to take a message with as much information in it as possible; remember, these were the days before voicemail and telephone recorders. She was asked to never say I was tied-up and to ask who was calling. She was instructed to say that I was out of the office and would return calls later in the day. Without exception, every call was returned that day unless it came in after 4 p.m., after which I allowed myself to return calls first thing the next morning. The discipline of managing phone calls made a terrific difference. I regained control over my time and could get things done on my list without being interrupted. By not telling clients I was tied-up and asking who was calling, they weren't led to believe some clients were more important than others.

The quiet hour rule evolved into a session in the conference room of the building next door where I could not be disturbed. I would take a salesman's catalog case full of policy files and work through endorsements, proposals, and new coverages without interruption, thereby making myself more efficient.

Planning lists became my primary time management tool. I used the Plan-Goals-and-Activities system (PGA), which set annual plans, specific goals, and weekly and daily activities. I was only modestly successful, however, until I resolved to make a major change. For months I would have a full "things to do" list for a day's work and begin working on the item that was the most pleasant or the easiest to accomplish. Important tasks were not getting done. Out of necessity, I began to apply a firm rule: arrange tasks from highest priority to least important and start working every day at the top of the list. Self-discipline coupled with prioritizing tasks made a huge difference in my productivity.

The second tool is to hire good people and delegate authority to them. For me, this lesson was learned the hard way. I was always worried no one else would service an account that I had produced as well as I could, and we would risk losing the account. I also worried about the opposite effect. Others might service an account all too well and take it away from me. These assumptions were dead wrong. When I sold my largest insurance agency to a regional brokerage, I reassigned two-thirds of my accounts to lieutenants. They took over the day-to-day service and renewal of those accounts, and to my astonishment, we did not lose a single one. The clients knew I was somewhere around if they needed me and they seemed to enjoy a more casual association.

By far my biggest fault was not hiring the best people I could find. Initially, I did not take the time to find high-quality personnel. I write "quality" because hiring just on a resume is a losing proposition. It was the character, values, and ambition of the individual that determined their effectiveness in the insurance agency. We could train a good person willing to learn, but a bad person already poorly trained was a liability. Surround yourself with good people, and they will make you more successful at the same time they reduce the burden on you. The extra time it takes to find them is an investment that will yield great dividends.

The third tool for good time management involves a critical assessment of your role in the business once it is scaled, making money, and sustainable. It's common knowledge that entrepreneurs are great at creating but aren't so adept at managing what they build. Michael Gerber, a small business expert, addressed this dichotomy in his book, *The E-Myth*, which is based on the simple idea that "small businesses are not started by business people." Entrepreneurs have technical or creative skills, but few have the requisite management skills to maintain a business over the long term. Gerber recommends developing systems the can produce consistent results, a kind of McDonalds-ization of the operation. When managers and systems are in place, the entrepreneur is freed up to do what he or she does best. Replacing yourself requires an overview and an understanding of every company operation. To that end, Gerber recommends the use of an organizational chart, and he insists that no matter how small a business is, it needs this chart. He assigns tactical work for the technicians and strategic work for the managers. See the chart on the next page.

Gerber also suggests, "Never create a game for your people that you're unwilling to play yourself." The highest compliment I ever received from one of my employees was that he did not mind working for me, because I worked harder than anyone else. Gerber says that while entrepreneurs start most businesses, the truth is many of them suffer from "entrepreneurial seizure" at some point. The E-Myth manager knows you do not organize people; instead, you organize work as a comprehensive system of responsibilities that enables the organization to function in the most effective, efficient, and predictable way possible. Gerber wants every entrepreneur to decide what the company should look like when it gets to where he or she wants it, and then work on the gap between the two.[35]

7 Steps in Your
Business
Development
Program

Systems Strategy

Marketing Strategy

People Strategy

Management Strategy

Organizational Strategy

Strategic Objective

Primary Aim

(Michael Gerber)

One of my favorite stories about systematizing a business comes from David Spire, a Bradenton, Florida business owner who has guest lectured in my entrepreneurship course. He built the premier IT computer business in his area by applying every systems idea he could find. Although his company installs and services sophisticated computer networks, Spire himself does not know the technical side of computer hardware or software. What he does know is how to standardize his business and take advantage of management concepts. He tells the story of trying to be all things to all people when he started. When he realized that 80 percent of his revenue was being generated by just 20 percent of his customers (the Pareto principle), Spire stopped serving retail, individual customers and began concentrating on commercial business customers only. His company,

---

[35] Michael E. Gerber, *The E-Myth Revisited,* (New York: Collins Business, 1995).

United Systems, could make turnkey, start-to-finish installations and then service them year-round on annual contracts. Spire's decision eliminated time wasting inquiries and unprofitable, single-person clients. Even his company's hiring practices were run through a system. When Spire sought to fill a position, he first tried to ascertain a candidate's social skills: "A lot of what I talk to them about is the relational aspect, how they handle themselves on the phone, what kind of answers they give. Once they get past that, we'll get them over to the technical side and vet them there."[36]

Takeaway from Chapter Twelve

Free yourself up by using timesaving strategies and by creating systems full of good people.

---

[36] David Spire, 2013, Presentation, ENT2000, State College of Florida.

CHAPTER THIRTEEN

The Plentiful Harvest

In seed time learn, in harvest teach, in winter enjoy.
— William Blake
Nineteenth-century English Poet and Artist

What I learned quite by accident is that a business you own that makes any money at all is valuable to someone. After only six months in business in Jacksonville, I was asked to lunch by the largest insurance brokerage in the city. They offered to buy my agency for a nice amount, and I was astonished that an offer came so early in my career. I was starting to cut into business sold the usual bureau company way. What they really wanted was my market and my relationship with it. As I wrote earlier, I was using a different business model and quoting a direct writer with an exclusive territory. I am quite sure this broker and others in town had tried to get a hold of Cotton States without success. The point is that any entity with an income stream has value and can be sold. I didn't sell at that time, but I tucked away this newly learned fact for future use.

Many years later after leaving the insurance industry and beginning an encore career as an educator, my best friend in Atlanta—we served in Vietnam together—needed some help. He had operated an employee benefits/ group health agency in a suburb of Atlanta for more than thirty years, and he had turned over much of the day-to-day operations to others. A recent employee had left with several house accounts and taken them to a competitor, which dealt my friend's business a serious blow. When I answered the call, I found my friend mentally stuck on what to do. His son, daughter-in-law, and a close family friend were working in the agency, and it was operating in the red for the first time. The solution, for a person who had built up and sold three insurance agencies, was easy to see. Whatever revenue remained (and there was a lot) was a valuable asset desired by many competitors. And what made this timing almost providential was that a few months earlier in Florida I had attended a health underwriters luncheon where a guest speaker from Atlanta solicited blocks of group health accounts for purchase.

I conducted the first few meetings alone as my friend recovered from understandable doldrums. We reached a point in the negotiations that actual money was to be discussed, and my friend came along with me to the meeting. During his presentation, the buyer made a pro forma calculation of possible purchase amounts on a whiteboard, and my buddy happily came alive. I was able to help a best friend with my knowledge of this valuable aspect of entrepreneurship: a business generating revenue has worth. Most businesses are bought using their own revenue as payments into the future. Thus, many purchases are structured based on the revenues over the buyout period and generally they do not hold the same level as when the entrepreneur was at the helm. I learned early on to sell only for a guaranteed cost or a set amount put into the sales contract. Understandably, the amount a buyer would pay is less for a guaranteed price, but the payout certainty was worth a lower multiple.

Businesses can be sold out of necessity or by choice. My first sale from Jacksonville was by choice to take advantage of an opportunity in another state, but the second sale of my largest agency was due to health issues. In some cases, businesses close because of bankruptcy or insufficient funds, perhaps expanding too quickly. In general, businesses can be sold outright for cash or a stock exchange, which has the benefit of being tax-free, and either inside the company or outside the company. Commonly, sales inside the company are either an ESOP (employee stock ownership plan) or an MBO (management buyout). An MBO is selling to existing partners or key managers. My last agency, a systemized insurance business involving only rural telephone companies in five southeastern states, was sold using the ESOP method. My two lieutenants bought equal amounts of company stock and ran the agency for ten years, at one point doubling its premium volume.

Selling outside the company can be a lengthy and costly process. There is a whole industry around selling businesses—business brokers, consultants, attorneys, and accountants—that charges for assistance. If an entrepreneur is not careful, these advisors end up with a large part of the sales proceeds. Among the options outside the company are mergers (join another company for shared growth), acquisition (sell to a major competitor or supplier), and strategic alliance (share resources with another company but retain autonomy). My first sale was to a major competitor; the second was to an out-of-town regional broker who needed an office in Atlanta, and the third was the ESOP.

The final way to harvest or exit your business is to go public. This method is the most sophisticated because it involves Security and Exchange Commission filings, lots of advisor work and fees, and loss of control of the business to public stockholders. Michael Dell lived to regret his initial public offering, or IPO, of Dell Computers and spent a lot of time and money buying his own company back. He wanted to revert his business to a private enterprise because he wanted to invest profits in product research, while the shareholders desired to maximize dividends. An IPO does offer several benefits. It can fund rapid growth, generate tremendous wealth—look at Mark Zuckerberg and Facebook—and explode marketing. Keep in mind, however, that going public is a lengthy and complex process that can be problematic.

Two key considerations in exiting a successful entrepreneurial business are timing and valuation. When you sell can be influenced by the markets you operate in and seasonal variations in revenues. With advance planning, a seller can select the best buyer and the time of year when revenues are at their highest. For example, my friend's employee benefits agency was sold just before full implementation of the Affordable Care Act, and the buyer had plans to operate as a regional exchange. He wanted to have as many accounts on his books as possible when the law took effect. Valuation is usually a formula based on some multiple of net earnings. Audited annual income statements are a key resource for marketing your company. If possible, obtain a professional valuation for your business to give credibility to your asking price. Potential buyers also want specific details about customer profiles and the assurance that key personnel will remain to ease the transition to new ownership. Above all, don't let your emotions keep you from accepting a fair deal. There are many new business opportunities awaiting you.

Negotiating the sale of a business can be a straightforward exercise, but it is wise to expect the unexpected. My experience selling my first company illustrates how important it is to pivot and use creativity to solve problems as they arise. Because I represented a direct writer that was a core part of my first insurance agency, any potential buyer had to have the blessing of Cotton States, the main carrier. Being busy and extremely naïve, I allowed the principals of the agency purchasing my business to make a trip to the Cotton States home office without me. When they returned to Jacksonville fully approved, they asked for a meeting to refine the sale agreement. My wife and I arrived, happy but clueless about our now disadvantaged bargaining position. The buyers wanted to reduce the amount of the agreement, knowing they had Cotton States' approval and that I was under a time constraint to get to California. Instead of a guaranteed price and the agreed upon multiple, they wanted a lower price and a payout over time. My reaction was not polite conversation, and we left in anger.

I spent the weekend trying to figure out what to do. The buyers thought they had me boxed in, because there was limited time to find another buyer. I recalled, however, that there was one other commercially oriented agent in Florida—Cotton States was primarily a personal lines insurer, i.e., auto and homeowner policies—located in Orlando. Its principal and I had socialized at an annual sales convention, and we were on cordial terms. Monday morning I called him and asked if he would simply say he wanted to buy my agency. To my surprise, he said he not only would say that but, in fact, if the deal fell through, he would be happy to buy my agency at the original terms. Armed with this backup offer, I refrained from contacting the original buyers. Days later as I worked in the early evening in my office, the owner of the independent agency originally buying my business called to chat. After some pleasantries, he asked what I was doing. I answered, "Working to complete a sale to an Orlando agency." Less than an hour later, he and his partner were in my office and the original deal was signed. You always want to negotiate from a position of strength and to be prepared for the unexpected.

My entrepreneur of choice for harvesting a startup is Bill Gates. He was born in Seattle in 1955 and began to show an interest in computers at age thirteen while attending the Lakeside School. A parents group had used proceeds from a rummage sale to purchase teletype terminals for students, and Gates and his friend Paul Allen spent all their spare time in the school's computer lab. Gates became interested with what computers could do. As a sophomore at Harvard, he devised an algorithm to solve a class problem, which remained the fastest solution for over thirty years. When the Altair 8800 computer kit was released in 1975, Gates and Allen saw it as an opportunity and opened their own computer software company. They named their partnership "Micro-Soft." Gates dropped out of college, and they returned to Seattle in 1979.

IBM approached Microsoft in 1980 looking for an operating system for their new personal computer, which Gates and Allen eventually provided after acquiring DOS from another Seattle computer company. Gates didn't transfer the copyright on the operating system because he believed other vendors would clone the system, which they did. MS-DOS made Microsoft the biggest player in the new personal computer industry, and they quickly expanded across the US and overseas. In 1984, Microsoft released Windows, a graphical extension of the DOS software, and went public. The rise in the stock as a result of the popularity of Windows, which made the DOS system operate most like Apple's graphical interface, went on to make four billionaires and some twelve thousand employees millionaires. After its March 1986 IPO, Microsoft's share price soared thirty-fold in eight years and peaked in December 1999 at $600 billion capitalization. As of 2006, Microsoft's two founders, Bill Gates and Paul Allen, still had the vast majority of their shares tied up in Microsoft (Gates at 45 percent and Allen at 25 percent) having long ago achieved billionaire status. In 2014, *Forbes* ranked Bill Gates the richest man in the world at $76 billion.

The Plentiful Harvest:

1. An entity with a revenue stream can be sold.
2. Most businesses are purchased using future income.
3. I learned to sell for less at a guaranteed price.
4. Sales inside the company are ESOPs and MBOs are management buy-outs.
5. The exit can be a merger, acquisition, or strategic alliance.
6. An Initial Public Offering (IPO) arises from rapid growth and has strict SEC requirements (certified audits).
7. Valuation is usually earning multiple using a benchmark (barrels sold) compared to like entities.

Takeaway from Chapter Thirteen

Don't procrastinate on planning an exit strategy. You need to factor in the best timing, your employees' needs, capital gains taxes, and your future plans.

CHAPTER FOURTEEN

Leaving Your Mark on the World

The purpose of the true social entrepreneur is to change the world.

— *Bill Drayton*
MacArthur Fellow and Chair of the Ashoka Foundation

Entrepreneurship is the lifeblood of an economy, and social entrepreneurs are particularly powerful today. These innovative people seek to solve social problems by combining business techniques with ingenuity and altruism. Jeremy Rifkin, an economist and bestselling author, writes about the future of social entrepreneurship in his latest book, *The Zero Marginal Cost Society*. Rifkin describes a paradigm shift that is happening as we automate whole sectors. He notes that even white-collar service industries are relying more and more on artificial intelligence, analytics, and voice recognition technologies. Work that formerly was done by humans is now being performed by algorithms and 3D printers. Rifkin is anything but pessimistic: "we are beginning to see that a mass surge of employment is migrating out of the market and into the social economy, the not-for-profit economy, where human social capital counts more than economic capital."[37]

One important factor explaining this shift is the aging of our country's population. Approximately 10,000 Baby Boomers are turning age sixty-five each day, which will continue for the next fifteen years. As this cohort of 76 million Americans gradually leaves the workforce, new opportunities for social entrepreneurs in leisure and cultural activities, sports and fitness

---

[37] Jeremy Rifkin, *Zero Marginal Cost Society*, (New York: Palgrave Macmillan, 2015).

programs, nutrition and healthcare, and related service industries will increase dramatically.

Another favorable factor for social entrepreneurship is the increasing importance of the millennial generation. Millennials are defined as the 75 million Americans born between 1981 and 1997, and this generation is not too interested in how things were done in the past.

Millennials are particularly attracted to innovation for the common good because they have been socialized in the world of the Internet. Collaboration is a key characteristic, and this method is supplanting the top-down management style of the previous generation. By adopting a teamwork approach, millennials can employ more diverse skill sets and apply broader perspectives for problem solving, especially when it involves improvements to the well-being of communities.

The increasing number of green enterprises evidences this trend. These startups create, invent, or organize products or services designed to save energy, recycle by-products, and/or reduce pollution. Examples include wind farming, solar panel installation, and carbon trading, which involves swapping carbon credits for the voluntary and the regulatory markets. In California, for example, an entire industry has developed after passage of strict carbon emission standards for licensed automobiles. Catalytic converters were required on any car sold in California by the EPA, but California created a cottage industry when they required even more efficient converters.

Social entrepreneurship is characterized by non-profit organizations, for-profit businesses, or government entities which focus on using resources to create social value. To illustrate their diversity, *Forbes* compiled a list of the Top 30 Social Entrepreneurs. These include Jordan Kassalow, an optometrist by trade who sells ready-made glasses to people in the developing world, Tom Skazy who dropped out of Princeton to create TerraCycle, which sells fertilizer made from sixty waste streams, and Jane Chen whose company manufactures a sleeping bag device called Thermpod, which warms low birth weight babies in settings with unreliable electricity.

The innovations of *Forbes*'s Top 30 range across health, education, finance, and other sectors such as the environment, energy, human resources, and community development. Some social products improve safety; others reduce pollution or improve the nutritional value of food. Social entrepreneurs are change agents who often invent a product to accomplish their mission. The Bill and Melinda Gates Foundation focuses on vaccines in third world countries as one of the most cost-effective health interventions. Because transportation systems and storage facilities are unreliable, it's difficult to preserve vaccines that require refrigeration. Using a Seattle-based inventor, Bill Gates created a large thermos capable of keeping immunizations cold for days. The Gates Foundation has also given energy companies grants to develop portable vaccine chillers for use in hot, remote areas where there is no reliable power supply.

One such company, True Energy located in Great Britain, started with a Gates Foundation grant and has since received millions in orders from UNICEF for refrigerators in Zimbabwe, Chad, and Ethiopia.

My favorite story of green entrepreneurship is the story of Big Belly, a solar-powered trash compactor invented by Jim Poss, an entrepreneurship graduate student from Babson College. He had a desire to do something green, and with his supervising professor, found function, practicality, and a positive market demand for a solar-powered trash compactor. Not only does Big Belly operate free of electricity, but it cuts the required dumpster pickups, and today there are more than 5,000 Big Bellies installed around the world. They hold up to five times the volume of ordinary trash receptacles, reduce greenhouse gases by 80 percent, and get 100 percent of their energy from the sun. Because they displace four out of five weekly trash pick-ups, they reduce transportation and labor costs.

Philadelphia now has 500 solar-powered trash receptacles. Over the next ten years, the city expects a net savings of over $13 million. Social entrepreneurs are also motivated by a desire to benefit succeeding generations. For-profit companies like Ben & Jerry's Ice Cream use some of their profits to fund charities. In 1978, Ben Cohen and Jerry Greenfield took a correspondence course on ice cream making, and with $12,000 they opened a store in a renovated gas station in Burlington, Vermont. Ben was particularly good at creating flavors, and their whimsical artwork and flavor names, combined with the idea of chunks mixed in with the ice cream, clicked with the public. In 1985, they established a foundation to fund 7.5 percent of pre-tax profits to community projects. Although today Ben & Jerry's is owned by Unilever, the Ben & Jerry's Foundation still provides funding for a number of philanthropic causes, and the corporation continues its earth-friendly manufacturing practices.

Another inspiring example is the company created by two engineers, Pettie Petzer and Johan Jonker. Their product, called the Hippo Roller, provides a better way for individuals to move water with much less effort from its source such as a well or stream to where it is consumed in homes. Nearly 50,000 Hippo Rollers, 95 percent of which have been donated, have been distributed to over twenty countries. More than 400,000 people have benefited from this innovation. It decreases traffic to and from water sources and it reduces spinal, back, and hand injuries. Based in Johannesburg, the company helps mostly Africans in developing countries.

Social enterprises innovate their startup capital as well. Because commercial lenders are not always willing to make loans to new and unproven businesses, entrepreneurs seek other avenues such as crowdfunding or peer-to-peer lending. Internet-based sites can pool capital from social investors who lend their money at moderate rates of return. Borrowers avoid the administrative overhead of traditional lenders, and funding can be expedited. Most startups using social lending sites are seeking loans in the $10,000 to $20,000 range. Three of the biggest lending sites are Prosper.com, Lending Club, and GreenNote. Another one is Kivo.org, a non-profit whose donors make zero-interest loans to causes they choose to support.

Few social ventures have lots of funding, so they need to focus on creativity, efficiency, and helping end-customers. Efficiency is needed to return as much money as possible to continue supporting the cause. Think of social entrepreneurship as having dual purposes: profitability combined with a social return. Areas to consider for potential social enterprise startups include creating and selling safe beauty products, educational travel programs, urban agriculture, and home healthcare consulting. Neil Blumenthal is the co-founder of Warby Parker, the eyewear startup he built by selling glasses for $95 a pair with a buy-one-give-one model, and he thinks the next big focus for social innovation is the public sector. In his opinion, "government and public policy are not moving at the pace of technology or even meeting expectations of constituents."[38] He hopes to see more products designed in the public interest to solve day-to-day issues like congested traffic. One place where this is happening is at Civic Hall, a co-working space in New York City dedicated to helping entrepreneurs build socially-minded companies to solve public problems. At the end of the day, social entrepreneurship is all about people helping people and having the satisfaction of knowing they are making the world a better place.

Takeaway from Chapter Fourteen

When you help others, you are really helping yourself.

---

[38] Catherine Clifford, "Warby Parker Co-Founder On The Next Generation Of Social Entrepreneurship," *Entrepreneur,* 2015, http://www.entrepreneur.com/article/243915.

CHAPTER FIFTEEN

What Are You Waiting For?

Do not wait until conditions are perfect to begin. Beginning makes the conditions perfect.

— *Alan Cohen*
Author of A Deep Breath of Life

Opportunity is all around us. It is in the unconventional, the changes that occur daily, the failure of others, or in a bold new way of doing things. Any keen observer who is open to new ideas is sure to spot emerging possibilities. As Jack Nadel has said, "Deals are like buses. There is always another one behind the one you just missed."[39] In many cases, a great idea may develop from the work you are already doing. In its research study, "The Entrepreneur Next Door," the Kauffman Foundation reported that people in the United States who already hold full- or part-time jobs are actually more likely to venture into entrepreneurship. In addition, the whole notion of a great idea may be overvalued. The execution of an idea is much more important for success.

The process of innovation almost always happens within a context. Breakthroughs large and small develop when needs present themselves and solutions arise in response to specific problems. I didn't reinvent the commercial insurance business, but I did apply the idea of combining a less expensive, direct writing insurance product with a higher quality, brokerage level service. This added an extra layer of value for the customer and provided a desirable niche for my business. Richard Branson made a

---

[39] Nadel, *Evolution of an Entrepreneur*, 111.

similar modification to carve out a unique position. He surprised trans-atlantic airline flyers when he took out first class seats on Virgin Atlantic Airlines. Branson had researched the market and felt confident that Virgin could earn more money using business class rather than first class. His airline continued innovating by adding more sleeper seats and airborne lounges as they stayed one step ahead of competition.

There are many reasons to give serious consideration to entrepreneurship and to having your own business. You get control over time, feel fulfillment, and can set your own salary. If you have a passion for doing something that makes money, working for yourself can be immensely rewarding. At this point, if you are serious about having your own business, continue to explore entrepreneurship by using the resources in the back of this book. Useful materials are all around you via online coursework, community college entrepreneurship programs, Small Business Administration startup tutorials, and the many Senior Corps of Retired Executives (SCORE) chapters spread across the country. The SCORE program provides free business coaching from successful entrepreneurs in all areas of commerce.

Overall, this book provides the framework, but it is up to you to add an entrepreneurial mindset and desire. The mindset is one of opportunity recognition and risk assumption. Let this book's guidelines inform your decisions, and if you stay the course, I promise you will experience a bountiful harvest. Without reservation I can say that the journey of self-employment is worth the experience. I have no regrets other than the reflection that a little more balance along the way might have been better. At this point in my career, the opportunity to serve small businesses, provide employment to good people, give protégés useful skills, and share my experiences delivers enormous satisfaction. I believe deeply in our capitalistic system that gives every person a shot at the brass ring. If you are willing to make a short-term sacrifice for a long-term reward, then now is the time to get started. In Peter Drucker's words, "Passion without action is to have the Ferrari in the garage collecting dust . . . the reality is those who take action win the race every time over those who don't."[40]

And if you think you are too old to try something new, consider Simon "Si" Ramo (the R in TRW Inc.). In 2013 at age 100, he received a patent for a computer-based learning invention, becoming the oldest person ever to receive a patent. Born in 1913, Ramo said he had always been interested in new ideas, and his name appears on dozens of patents. Among his many awards, he received the Presidential Medal of Freedom. Obviously, Ramo is an inspiration to both young and mature workers who are considering becoming entrepreneurs. He passed away in 2014 but left a wonderful legacy behind.

The next step is up to you. I suggest you launch your entrepreneurial adventure with a blank sheet of paper and a pen. Write down your initial ideas and goals, because that's how a successful business begins. What are you good at doing? What are your passions? And what experience have you had in commercial business? If you build the desire, send out a cause, generate ideas, look for opportunities, find a willing mentor, develop people skills, and are willing to assume minimal risk, then you too can become a successful entrepreneur and **set your own salary**.

Takeaway from Chapter Fifteen

The best way to predict your future is to create it.

---

[40] Eric T. Wagner, "Entrepreneurship According to Drucker: Your 12 Keys to Success," *Forbes,* 2013, http://www.forbes.com/sites/ericwagner/2013/05/07/entrepreneurship-according-to-drucker-your-12-keys-to-success/.

The Entrepreneurship Map

By Clinton E. Day, Entrepreneurship Adjunct Professor

Mindset - The entrepreneurial mindset is marked by imagination, initiative, and a readiness to undertake new projects. It is perseverance, determination, risk-taking and opportunity recognition.
Desire.

Commerce – Global economy, flow of goods and services combined with the need for a product or service in demand by a targeted segment of customers.
Need.

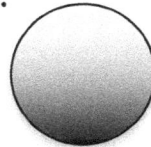

Idea – Opportunity, problem, observation, innovation, serendipity, intuitive hunch.
Niche.

Feasibility – Viable, niched product or service with a competitive advantage and financial utility as reviewed by SWOT and industry analysis.
Test.

Action – Lean Startup or Smart Step with resources at hand just acting which "trumps everything." "Creaction" searches for a business model many times until a successful approach is found.

Launch.

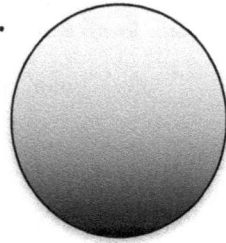

Adjust – Research, listen to potential customers over and over, pivot, iterate, and change strategy until the idea clicks. Classic business plan is needed once sustainability has been reached.

Certainty.

New Venture FOUNDATION

Fund – Bootstrapping, debt/equity financing, investors, VCs.

Build – Sacrifice, team, delegate, TQM, MBO, economic impact.

Exit – Partner, sell, merge, setup ESOP or IPO.

Resources

A. Business Owner's Tool Kit (know how for small business entrepreneurs).

B. Chambers of Commerce (US Chamber and local websites).

C. Consortium for Entrepreneurship Education (sharing of professional articles).

D. DOL, Department of Labor (bureau of labor statistics, secondary research).

E. Entrepreneur magazine and website (entrepreneur.com).

F. Foundation for Enterprise Development (entrepreneurship and innovation materials).

G. Harvard Business School's entrepreneurship resources (hbs.edu).

H. IFA, International Franchise Association (resource of 1,200 franchisors).

I. Industry trade associations (Encyclopedia of Associations, Gale Directory/Lexis).

J. MOCCs (free online courses: Udacity, Coursera, Babson, MIT, Carnegie-Mellon).

K. NACCE (National Association for Community College Entrepreneurship) local education.

L. NBIA, National Business Incubator Association (for local entrepreneurship centers).

M. NFTE, Network for Teaching Entrepreneurship (for K12 entrepreneurship).

N. SBA, Small Business Administration (website sba.gov, startup business tutorial).

O. SBDC, Small Business Development Centers network (state, SBA, universities amalgam).

P. SCORE, Senior Corps of Retired Executives (free or low-cost small business advice).

Q. Stanford Technology Ventures Program (textbook, syllabi, cases).

R. Startup Nation (resource and information for starting a small business, startupnation.com).

S. USASBE, US Association for Small Businesses & Entrepreneurship (advances education and research).

T. US Department of State, Bureau of International Information Programs (principles of entrepreneurship).

Glossary of Terms

Accelerator: Organization that supports startup business by providing a support location.

Acquisition cost: Total cost of acquiring an asset including purchase, transportation, testing, etc.

Balance sheet: Overall financial picture of a new business and a forecasting source.

Bootstrapping: Using pre-existing, privately owned resources other than borrowed money.

BATNA: Best alternative to a negotiated settlement; a strategy to use when negotiations fail.

Book value: Difference between original acquisition cost and accumulated depreciation.

Breakeven point: When a startup business reaches the point where income equals expense.

Burn rate: Rate at which a company spends its capital until it reaches profitability.

Business incubator: Public or private entrepreneurial organization to support wannabe entrepreneurs.

Business plan: A written document describing aspects of a business venture necessary to raise money.

Competitive advantage: Way a firm implements customer benefits to keep it ahead of competitive firms.

Copyright: Exclusive right given the creator of a literary or artistic work to use that work.

Corporation: A legal, artificial entity that is formed by filing documents with a state government.

Cost/benefit analysis: A decision making process in which the costs of taking action are compared to benefits.

CreAction: Babson College term for acting and creating evidence in the entrepreneurial process (Schlesinger).

Creativity: A process producing an idea or opportunity that is novel and useful.

Creative destruction: Process by which new product/technologies make current products obsolete.

Crowdfunding: Funding a business through collective, private investments over the Internet.

Current ratio: Value of current assets divided by current liabilities.

Design patent: A 14-year patent for a new, original, and ornamental design for an article of manufacture.

Differentiation strategy: A strategy that firms use to provide unique or different products to consumers.

Direct marketing: Selling goods or services to consumers without intermediaries.

Due diligence: Process of investigating a business to determine its value.

Early adopters: A customer adoption segment that purchases after pioneers.

Economic value: What startup ventures create out of useful ideas for the benefit of everyone.

Economies of scale: Idea that it is cheaper to make many of an item, mass producing a product.

Effectuation: An entrepreneurial approach that emphasizes creating opportunity by leveraging existing resources.

Elasticity: An economic term that describes the relationship between changes in two variables (price v. sales).

Entrepreneur: A person who owns or starts a business and is willing to risk loss in order to make money.

Elevator pitch: A brief, carefully constructed explanation of the merits of a business opportunity.

Equity: Ownership of business.

ESOP: Employee stock option plan; method for employees to purchase the business where they work.

ETA: Entrepreneurial thought in action, a Babson College term for the prediction and creation process.

Executive summary: Most important section of the business plan running one to two pages and overviews the business, its business model, market, and goals.

Factoring: Transaction where a business sells its accounts receivables to a third party at a discount for cash.

Fast track program: A provision in the SBIR program that combines phases into a grant. At the Kauffman Foundation FastTrac is a mentoring and sharing of ideas program.

Feasibility: Examination including finances of a business idea to determine how viable and realistic it is.

Fiduciary: Relating to or involving a confidence or trust between a trustee and a beneficiary.

Financials, entrepreneurship: Key statements are balance sheet, income statement, and statement of cash flows.

Fixed costs: Costs that do not change with an increase or decrease in the amount of goods produced.

Franchising: A form of business organization in which a firm already successful licenses its trademark and methods of doing business in exchange for a fee and ongoing revenue.

Gazelle: Fast growing company with annual growth of 20 percent or greater.

Green entrepreneurship: Running a firm in a manner that saves or improves the environment.

Improvisation: Creating action without pre-planning, impromptu, done without preparation.

Income statement: A financial statement that reflects the operations of a firm over a period of time.

Incubator: An entrepreneurship center, public or private, that allows collaboration of startup businesses.

Industry analysis: Along with the feasibility analysis used to consider entry costs and the competitive picture.

Intellectual property: Legal protections for what has been created—copyrights, trademarks, and patents.

Iteration: In lean methodology a minor change of a current business model.

Innovation: Process of creating something new.

Lean methodology: Search for a business model that works through frequent customer feedback (Blank).

IPO: Initial Public Offering; First time public sale of stock listed on an exchange.

License: A legal agreement granting rights to use a particular piece of intellectual property.

Lifecycle: Stages of an industry from birth to end, introduction, growth, maturity, decline and death.

Life-style entrepreneurs: Motivated by independence, meaningful work, and a desire to be in charge.

LLC: Limited Liability Company; A form of business organization that combines the limited liability of a corporation with the tax advantages of a partnership.

Market segmentation: Studying the industry in which the firm intends to compete to determine the target markets.

Minimum viable product (MVP): The smallest thing you can build that delivers customer value (Ries).

Mission statement: Describes why the business exists and what its business model should accomplish.

Moral hazard: Problem firm faces as it grows and adds personnel, new hires do not have the same incentives.

Nascent entrepreneurs: One or more persons start to commit time and resources to starting a new firm.

Niche market: A place within a large market segment that represents a narrow group of customers.

Opportunity cost: Cost of passing up the next best alternative when making a decision.

Opportunity recognition: Process of perceiving the possibility of a profitable new product or service.

Outsourcing: Work that is done for a company by people other than the company employees.

Owner's equity: Difference between assets and liabilities of a business.

Patent: Grant from the federal government conferring rights to exclude others.

Pivot: In lean methodology a wholesale change of a current business model.

P/E: price/earnings ratio; Measures the price of a company's stock against its earnings.

Prior art: Information available to the public before a date relevant to a claim for originality.

Profit margin: The markup or percentage of a selling price that is profit.

Pro forma financial statement: Shows a projected picture of a company's assets, liabilities, and owner's equity at a specific time.

ROI: return on investment; A capital budget item used to measure the relationship between initial investment and profits that are expected.

SBA guaranteed loan program: Source of funding for small businesses in which bank participation is 50 percent.

SBIR program: Small business innovation research competitive grant program that provides funding for early stage technology development.

Scalability: Ability for a business or technology to accept increased volume, grow revenue faster than costs; when the business model has succeeded and profits are flowing.

Serial entrepreneurs: People who open multiple businesses throughout their career.

Smart step: A small, first step to begin the entrepreneurial learning process coined by Babson College.

SMEs: Small and medium enterprises.

Social entrepreneurship: Motivated by a greater good, the return to society; can be for-profit or non-profit.

Statement of cash flows: Financial statement summarizing the changes in a firm's cash position for a period.

STTR program: A government program that requires the participation of a research organization.

Supply chain: Line of distribution of a product from its start to its handling by customers.

Surety Bond: Used in public bidding, a three-party agreement that legally binds the principal, the obligee (who requires the bond), and a surety company to a contract's successful execution.

Sustainability: The ability to survive long enough to generate a return on investment.

Sustainable entrepreneurship: Starting, running a firm in a manner which saves or improves the environment.

Target market: A limited group that a firm goes after, the focus of promotion and sales efforts.

Trademark: Distinctive word, slogan, or image that identifies a product and its origin.

Variable costs: Costs that change with each unit produced (e. g., raw materials).

Venture capital: Funding provided startup companies with high potential often during their second stage.

Window of opportunity: Time period in which a firm or an entrepreneur can realistically enter a new market.

Working capital: A firm's current (less than one year) assets minus its current liabilities.

Bibliography

Anderson, Chris. "Elon Musk's Mission to Mars." *Wired*. 2012. http://www.wired.com/2012/10/ff-elon-musk-qa/.

Beesley, Caron. "Why A Mentor Is Key To Small Business Growth And Survival." *SBA.gov*. 2014. https://www.sba.gov/blogs/why-mentor-key-small-business-growth-and-survival-0.

Bibb, Porter. *Ted Turner: It Ain't as Easy as It Looks.* Boulder, CO: Johnson Books, 1997.

Carnegie, Dale. *How to Stop Worrying and Start Living.* New York: Pocket Books, 1985.

Carnegie, Dale. *How to Win Friends and Influence People.* New York: Pocket Books, 1998.

Christensen, Clayton M., and Michael E. Raynor. *The Innovator's Solution: Creating and Sustaining Successful Growth.* Boston, Massachusetts: Harvard Business Review Press, 2013.

Clifford, Catherine. 2015. "Warby Parker Co-Founder on The Next Generation of Social Entrepreneurship." *Entrepreneur*. http://www.entrepreneur.com/article/243915.

Covey, Stephen R. *The 7 Habits of Highly Effective People.* New York: Free Press, 2004.

Csikszentmihalyi, Mihaly. *Creativity: The Psychology of Discovery and Invention.* New York: Harper Perennial Modern Classics, 2013.

Dahl, Darren. "How to Build Better Business Relationships." *Inc.* 2011. http://www.inc.com/guides/201101/how-to-build-better-business-relationships.html.

Dell, Michael S. "2003 University Of Texas at Austin Commencement Address." Speech, University of Texas at Austin, 2003.

Drucker, Peter F. *Innovation and Entrepreneurship: Practice and Principles.* New York: HarperBusiness, 1993.

Ewing Marion Kauffman Foundation. "Our Founder." 2015. http://www.kauffman.org/who-we-are/our-founder-ewing-kauffman.

Fidelity Charitable Gift Fund. *Entrepreneurs Are More Likely To Give To Charity.* 2010. http://www.fidelitycharitable.org/about-us/news/11-12-2010.shtml.

Fisher, Roger, William Ury, and Bruce Patton. *Getting to Yes: Negotiating Agreement without Giving In.* New York: Penguin, 2011.

Gerber, Michael E. *The E-Myth Revisited.* New York: CollinsBusiness, 1995.

Getty, J P. *How to Be Rich.* New York: Jove Books, 1983.

Hill, Napoleon. *Think and Grow Rich.* Radford, VA: Wilder Publications, 2007.

Hills, G.E., Shrader, R.C. and Lumpkin, G.T. "Opportunity recognition as a creative process." *Frontiers of Entrepreneurship Research.* Babson College, Wellesley, MA, 1999.

Howard, Fred. *Wilbur and Orville: A Biography of the Wright Brothers.* Mineola, N.Y: Dover Publications, 1998.

Kiefer, Charles F., Leonard A. Schlesinger, and Paul B. Brown. *Action Trumps Everything: Creating What You Want in an Uncertain World.* Duxbury, MA: Black Ink Press, 2010.

Krug, Steve. *Don't Make Me Think, Revisited: A Common Sense Approach to Web Usability.* San Francisco, CA: New Riders, Peachpit, Pearson Education, 2014.

Maltz, Maxwell. *Psycho-Cybernetics: A New Way to Get More Living Out of Life.* New York: Pocket Books, 1989.

Michalko, Michael. "Thomas Edison's Creative Thinking Habits." *Creative Thinking.* 2013. http://creativethinking.net/thomas-edisons-creative-thinking-habits/#sthash.dJXZImcY.mI7GX5je.dpbs.

Nadel, Jack. *The Evolution of an Entrepreneur.* Santa Monica, CA: JNJ Publishing, LLC, 2013.

Newlands, Murray. "Top 5 Wed-Apps Pivoting the Huge Wedding Industry." *Inc.* 2014. http://www.inc.com/murray-newlands/top-5-wed-apps-pivoting-the-300b-wedding-industry.html.

Popular Mechanics. "101 Gadgets That Changed the World." 2011. http://www.popularmechanics.com/technology/gadgets/reviews/g165/101-gadgets-that-changed-the-world/?slide=101.

Rifkin, Jeremy. *Zero Marginal Cost Society.* New York: Palgrave Macmillan, 2015.

Schwartz, David J. *The Magic of Thinking Big.* New York: Simon & Schuster, 1987.

Spire, David. 2013. Presentation. ENT2000, State College of Florida.

Wagner, Eric T. "Entrepreneurship According to Drucker: Your 12 Keys to Success." *Forbes.* 2013. http://www.forbes.com/sites/ericwagner/2013/05/07/entrepreneurship-according-to-drucker-your-12-keys-to-success/.

Weisman, Aly. "Ted Turner Reveals His Biggest Business Regret With CNN." *Business Insider.* 2012. http://www.businessinsider.com/ted-turner-wishes-cnn-had-less-fluff-2012-10.

Williams, Andy. *SEO 2015 & Beyond.* Charleston, SC: CreateSpace Independent Publishing Platform, 2014.

About the Author

Clint Day is an adjunct business professor who guest lectures to entrepreneurship programs. He is a serial entrepreneur who founded three insurance entities in Florida and Georgia and began teaching/mentoring after selling his last business. Professionally qualified by the AACSB business school association, Clint holds bachelor degrees from UC Berkeley and Eckerd College and a MBA in entrepreneurship from Salve Regina University. Certified by the Babson SEE, Kauffman Ice House and FastTrack, NCIIA Lean LaunchPad, UF Experiential Classroom, and Network for Teaching Entrepreneurship courses, Clint wrote the Entrepreneurship Quick Study Guide found in most college bookstores, is a member of the NACCE and USASBE associations and publishes the long running Current in Entrepreneurship blog on setyourownsalary.com/blog.

More about the author at:
http://www.linkedin.com/in/clintday/.
https://setyourownsalary.com/about.
https://Moneybyday.com.

*The Bar Charts Quick Study Guide on Entrepreneurship can be ordered online http://amazon.com/author/clintonday for $6.95.